Memoirs of Casanova Volume XII

Memoirs of Casanova Volume XII

Giacomo Casanova

MINT EDITIONS

Memoirs of Casanova Volume XII was first published in 1902.

This edition published by Mint Editions 2021.

ISBN 9781513281940 | E-ISBN 9781513286969

Published by Mint Editions®

MINT EDITIONS

minteditionbooks.com

Publishing Director: Jennifer Newens
Design & Production: Rachel Lopez Metzger
Project Manager: Micaela Clark
Translated By: Arthur Machen
Typesetting: Westchester Publishing Services

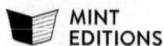

Contents

I

My Fortune in Holland—My Return to Paris with Young Pompeati

Amongst the letters which were waiting for me was one from the comptroller-general, which advised me that twenty millions in Government securities had been placed in the hands of M. d'Afri, who was not to go beyond a loss of eight per cent.; and another letter from my good patron, M. de Bernis, telling me to do the best I could, and to be assured that the ambassador would be instructed to consent to whatever bargain might be made, provided the rate was not more disadvantageous than that of the exchange at Paris. Boaz, who was astonished at the bargain I had made with my shares, wanted to discount the Government securities for me, and I should very likely have agreed to his terms if he had not required me to give him three months, and the promise that the agreement should hold even in the case of peace being concluded in the meanwhile. It was not long before I saw that I should do well to get back to Amsterdam, but I did not care to break my word to Therese, whom I had promised to meet at the Hague. I received a letter from her while I was at the play, and the servant who brought it told me he was waiting to conduct me to her. I sent my own servant home, and set out on my quest.

My guide made me climb to the fourth floor of a somewhat wretched house, and there I found this strange woman in a small room, attended by her son and daughter. The table stood in the midst of the room, and was covered with a black cloth, and the two candles standing upon it made it look like some sort of sepulchral altar. The Hague was a Court town. I was richly dressed; my elaborate attire made the saddest possible contrast with the gloom of my surroundings. Therese, dressed in black and seated between her children at that black table, reminded me of Medea. To see these two fair young creatures vowed to a lot of misery and disgrace was a sad and touching sight. I took the boy between my arms, and pressing him to my breast called him my son. His mother told him to look upon me as his father from henceforth. The lad recognized me; he remembered, much to my delight, seeing me in the May of 1753, in Venice, at Madame Manzoni's. He was slight but strong; his limbs were well proportioned, and his features intellectual. He was thirteen years old.

His sister sat perfectly still, apparently waiting for her turn to come. I took her on my knee, and as I embraced her, nature herself seemed to tell me that she was my daughter. She took my kisses in silence, but it was easy to see that she thought herself preferred to her brother, and was charmed with the idea. All her clothing was a slight frock, and I was able to feel every limb and to kiss her pretty little body all over, delighted that so sweet a being owed her existence to me.

"Mamma, dear," said she, "is not this fine gentleman the same we saw at Amsterdam, and who was taken for my papa because I am like him? But that cannot be, for my papa is dead."

"So he is, sweetheart; but I may be your dear friend, mayn't I? Would you like to have me for a friend?"

"Yes, yes!" she cried, and throwing her arms about my neck gave me a thousand kisses, which I returned with delight.

After we had talked and laughed together we sat down at table, and the heroine Therese gave me a delicate supper accompanied by exquisite wines. "I have never given the margrave better fare," said she, "at those nice little suppers we used to take together."

Wishing to probe the disposition of her son, whom I had engaged to take away with me, I addressed several remarks to him, and soon discovered that he was of a false and deceitful nature, always on his guard, taking care of what he said, and consequently speaking only from his head and not from his heart. Every word was delivered with a quiet politeness which, no doubt, was intended to please me.

I told him that this sort of thing was all very well on occasion; but that there were times when a man's happiness depended on his freedom from constraint; then and only then was his amiability, if he had any, displayed. His mother, thinking to praise him, told me that reserve was his chief characteristic, that she had trained him to keep his counsel at all times and places, and that she was thus used to his being reserved with her as with everyone else.

"All I can say is," said I, "your system is an abominable one. You may have strangled in their infancy all the finer qualities with which nature has endowed your son, and have fairly set him on the way to become a monster instead of an angel. I don't see how the most devoted father can possibly have any affection for a son who keeps all his emotions under lock and key."

This outburst, which proceeded from the tenderness I would fain have felt for the boy, seemed to strike his mother dumb.

"Tell me, my dear, if you feel yourself capable of shewing me that confidence which a father has a right to expect of a good son, and if you can promise to be perfectly open and unreserved towards me?"

"I promise that I will die rather than tell you a falsehood."

"That's just like him," said the mother. "I have succeeded in inspiring him with the utmost horror of untruthfulness."

"That's all very well, my dear madam, but you might have pursued a still better course, and one which would have been still more conducive to his happiness."

"What is that?"

"I will tell you. It was necessary to make him detest a lie; you should have rather endeavoured to make him a lover of the truth by displaying it to him in all its native beauty. This is the only way to make him lovable, and love is the sole bestower of happiness in this world."

"But isn't it the same thing not to lie and to tell the truth," said the boy, with a smile which charmed his mother and displeased me.

"Certainly not; there is a great difference—for to avoid lying you have only to hold your tongue; and do you think that comes to the same thing as speaking the truth? You must open your mind to me, my son, and tell me all your thoughts, even if you blush in the recital. I will teach you how to blush, and soon you will have nothing to fear in laying open all your thoughts and deeds. When we know each other a little longer we shall see how we agree together. You must understand that I cannot look upon you as my son until I see cause to love you, and I cannot have you call me father till you treat me as the best friend you have. You may be quite sure that I shall find a way to discover your thoughts, however cleverly you try to hide them. If I find you deceitful and suspicious I shall certainly entertain no regard for you. As soon as I have finished my business at Amsterdam we will set out for Paris. I am leaving the Hague to-morrow, and on my return I hope to find you instructed by your mother in a system of morality more consonant with my views, and more likely to lead to your happiness."

On glancing at my little daughter, who had been listening to me with the greatest attention, I saw that her eyes were swimming with tears, which she could hardly retain.

"Why are you crying?" said the mother; "it is silly to cry." And with that the child ran to her mother and threw her arms round her neck.

"Would you like to come to Paris, too?" said I to her.

"Oh, yes! But mamma must come too, as she would die without me."

"What would you do if I told you to go?" said the mother.

"I would obey you, mamma, but how could I exist away from you?"

Thereupon my little daughter pretended to cry. I say pretended, as it was quite evident that the child did not mean what she said, and I am sure that her mother knew it as well as I.

It was really a melancholy thing to see the effects of a bad education on this young child, to whom nature had given intelligence and feeling. I took the mother on one side, and said that if she had intended to make actors of her children she had succeeded to admiration; but if she wished them to become useful members of society her system had failed lamentably, as they were in a fair way to become monsters of deceit. I continued making her the most pointed remonstrances until, in spite of her efforts to control herself, she burst into tears. However, she soon recovered her composure, and begged me to stay at the Hague a day longer, but I told her it was out of the question, and left the room. I came in again a few minutes after, and Sophie came up to me and said, in a loving little voice,

"If you are really my friend, you will give me some proof of your friendship."

"And what proof do you want, my dear?"

"I want you to come and sup with me to-morrow."

"I can't, Sophie dear, for I have just said no to your mother, and she would be offended if I granted you what I had refused her."

"Oh, no! she wouldn't; it was she who told me to ask you just now."

I naturally began to laugh, but on her mother calling the girl a little fool, and the brother adding that he had never committed such an indiscretion, the poor child began to tremble all over, and looked abashed. I reassured her as best I could, not caring whether what I said displeased her mother or not, and I endeavoured to instill into her principles of a very different nature to those in which she had been reared, while she listened with an eagerness which proved that her heart was still ready to learn the right way. Little by little her face cleared, and I saw that I had made an impression, and though I could not flatter myself that any good I might do her would be lasting in its effects as long as she remained under the bad influence of her mother, I promised to come and sup with her next evening, "but on the condition," I said, "that you give me a plain meal, and one bottle of chambertin only, for you are not too well off."

"I know that, but mamma says that you pay for everything."

This reply made me go off into a roar of laughter; and in spite of her vexation the mother was obliged to follow my example. The poor woman, hardened by the life she led, took the child's simplicity for stupidity, but I saw in her a rough diamond which only wanted polishing.

Therese told me that the wine did not cost her anything, as the son of the Rotterdam burgomaster furnished her with it, and that he would sup with us the next day if I would allow him to be present. I answered smilingly that I should be delighted to see him, and I went away after giving my daughter, of whom I felt fond, a tender embrace. I would have done anything to be entrusted with her, but I saw it would be no good trying to get possession of her, as the mother was evidently keeping her as a resource for her old age. This is a common way for adventuresses to look upon their daughters, and Therese was an adventuress in the widest acceptation of the term. I gave her twenty ducats to get clothes for my adopted son and Sophie, who, with spontaneous gratitude, and her eyes filled with tears, came and gave me a kiss. Joseph was going to kiss my hand, but I told him that it was degrading for one man to kiss another's hand, and that for the future he was to shew his gratitude by embracing me as a son embraces his father.

Just as I was leaving, Therese took me to the closet where the two children were sleeping. I knew what she was thinking of; but all that was over long ago; I could think of no one but Esther.

The next day I found the burgomaster's son at my actress's house. He was a fine young fellow of twenty or twenty-one, but totally devoid of manner. He was Therese's lover, but he should have regulated his behaviour in my presence. Therese, seeing that he was posing as master of the field, and that his manners disgusted me, began to snub him, much to his displeasure, and after sneering at the poorness of the dishes, and praising the wine which he had supplied, he went out leaving us to finish our dessert by ourselves. I left myself at eleven, telling Therese that I should see her again before I went away. The Princesse de Galitzin, a Cantimir by birth, had asked me to dinner, and this made me lose another day.

Next day I heard from Madame d'Urfe, who enclosed a bill of exchange on Boaz for twelve thousand francs. She said that she had bought her shares for sixty thousand, that she did not wish to make anything of them, and that she hoped I would accept the overplus as my broker's fee. She worded her offer with too much courtesy for me to refuse it. The remainder of the letter was devoted to the wildest fancies. She said that her genius had revealed to her that I should bring back to Paris a boy born of the Mystical Marriage, and she hoped I would take pity on her. It was a strange coincidence, and seemed likely to attach the woman still more closely to her visionary theories. I laughed when I though how she would be impressed by Therese's son, who was certainly not born of the Mystical Marriage.

Boaz paid me my twelve thousand francs in ducats, and I made him my friend, as he thanked me for receiving the moneys in ducats, and he doubtless made a profit on the transaction, gold being a commodity in Holland, and all payments being made in silver or paper money.

At that time gold was at a low rate, and nobody would take ducats.

After having an excellent dinner with the Princesse de Galitzin, I put on my cloak and went to the cafe. I found there the burgomaster's son, who was just beginning a game of billiards. He whispered to me that I might back him with advantage, and thinking he was sure of his stroke I thanked him and followed his advice. However, after losing three games one after the other, I took his measure and began to lay against him without his knowledge. After playing for three hours and losing all the time, he stopped play and came to condole with me on my heavy loss. It is impossible to describe his amazed expression when I shewed him a handful of ducats, and assured him that I had spent a very profitable evening in laying against him. Everybody in the room began to laugh at him, but he was the sort of young man who doesn't understand a joke, and he went out in a rage. Soon after I left the billiard-room myself, and, according to my promise went to see Therese, as I was leaving for Amsterdam the next day.

Therese was waiting for her young wine merchant, but on my recounting his adventures she expected him no longer. I took my little daughter on my knee and lavished my caresses on her, and so left them, telling them that we should see each other again in the course of three weeks or a month at latest.

As I was going home in the moonlight by myself, my sword under my arm, I was encountered all of a sudden by the poor dupe of a burgomaster's son.

"I want to know," said he, "if your sword has as sharp a point as your tongue."

I tried to quiet him by speaking common sense, and I kept my sword wrapped in my cloak, though his was bared and directed against me.

"You are wrong to take my jests in such bad part," said I; "however, I apologize to you."

"No apologies; look to yourself."

"Wait till to-morrow, you will be cooler then, but if you still wish it I will give you satisfaction in the midst of the billiard-room."

"The only satisfaction you can give me is to fight; I want to kill you."

As evidence of his determination, and to provoke me beyond recall, he struck me with the flat of his sword, the first and last time in my life in which I have received such and insult. I drew my sword, but still hoping to bring him to his senses I kept strictly on the defensive and endeavoured to make him leave off. This conduct the Dutchman mistook for fear, and pushed hard on me, lunging in a manner that made me look to myself. His sword passed through my necktie; a quarter of an inch farther in would have done my business.

I leapt to one side, and, my danger no longer admitting of my fighting on the defensive, I lunged out and wounded him in the chest. I thought this would have been enough for him, so I proposed we should terminate our engagement.

"I'm not dead yet," said he; "I want to kill you."

This was his watchword; and, as he leapt on me in a paroxysm of rage, more like a madman than a sensible being, I hit him four times. At the fourth wound he stepped back, and, saying he had had enough, begged me to leave him.

I went off as fast as I could, and was very glad to see from the look of my sword that his wounds were slight. I found Boaz still up, and on hearing what had taken place he advised me to go to Amsterdam at once, though I assured him that the wounds were not mortal. I gave in to his advice, and as my carriage was at the saddler's he lent me his, and I set out, bidding my servant to come on the next day with my luggage, and to rejoin me at the "Old Bible," in Amsterdam. I reached Amsterdam at noon and my man arrived in the evening.

I was curious to hear if my duel had made any noise, but as my servant had left at an early hour he had heard nothing about it. Fortunately for me nothing whatever was known about it at Amsterdam for a week after; otherwise, things might not have gone well with me, as the reputation of being a duellist is not a recommendation to financiers with whom one is about to transact business of importance.

The reader will not be surprised when I tell him that my first call was on M. d'O, or rather on his charming daughter Esther, for she it was on whom I waited. It will be remembered that the way in which we parted did a good deal towards augmenting the warmth of my affection for her. On entering the room I found Esther writing at a table.

"What are you doing Esther, dear?"

"An arithmetical problem."

"Do you like problems?"

"I am passionately fond of anything which contains difficulties and offers curious results."

"I will give you something which will please you."

I made her, by way of jest, two magic squares, which delighted her. In return, she spewed me some trifles with which I was well acquainted, but which I pretended to think very astonishing. My good genius then inspired me with the idea of trying divination by the cabala. I told her to ask a question in writing, and assured her that by a certain kind of calculation a satisfactory answer would be obtained. She smiled, and asked why I had returned to Amsterdam so soon. I shewed her how to make the pyramid with the proper numbers and the other ceremonies, then I made her extract the answer in numbers, translating it into French, and greatly was she surprised to find that the cause which had made me return to Amsterdam so soon was—love.

Quite confounded, she said it was very wonderful, even though the answer might not be true, and she wished to know what masters could teach this mode of calculation.

"Those who know it cannot teach it to anyone."

"How did you learn it, then?"

"From a precious manuscript I inherited from my father."

"Sell it me."

"I have burnt it; and I am not empowered to communicate the secret to anyone before I reach the age of fifty."

"Why fifty?"

"I don't know; but I do know that if I communicated it to anyone before that age I should run the risk of losing it myself. The elementary spirit who is attached to the oracle would leave it."

"How do you know that?"

"I saw it so stated in the manuscript I have spoken of."

"Then you are able to discover all secrets?"

"Yes, or I should be if the replies were not sometimes too obscure to be understood."

"As it does not take much time, will you be kind enough to get me an answer to another question?"

"With pleasure; you can command me in anything not forbidden by my familiar spirit."

She asked what her destiny would be, and the oracle replied that she had not yet taken the first step towards it. Esther was astonished and called her governess to see the two answers, but the good woman saw nothing wonderful in them whatever. Esther impatiently called her a blockhead, and entreated me to let her ask another question. I begged her to do so, and she asked,

"Who loves me most in Amsterdam?" The oracle replied that no one loved her as well as he who had given her being: Poor Esther then told me that I had made her miserable, and that she would die of grief if she could not succeed in learning the method of calculation. I gave no answer, and pretended to feel sad at heart. She began to write down another question, putting her hand in front so as to screen the paper. I rose as if to get out of her way, but while she was arranging the pyramid I cast my eyes on the paper whilst walking up and down the room, and read her question. After she had gone as far as I had taught her, she asked me to extract the answer, saying that I could do so without reading the question. I agreed to do so on the condition that she would not ask a second time.

As I had seen her question, it was easy for me to answer it. She had asked the oracle if she might shew the questions she had propounded to her father, and the answer was that she would be happy as long as she had no secrets from her father.

When she read these words she gave a cry of surprise, and could find no words wherewith to express her gratitude to me. I left her for the Exchange, where I had a long business conversation with M. Pels.

Next morning a handsome and gentlemanly man came with a letter of introduction from Therese, who told me that he would be useful in case I wanted any assistance in business. His name was Rigerboos. She informed me that the burgomaster's son was only slightly wounded, and that I had nothing to fear as the matter was not generally known, and that if I had business at the Hague I might return there in perfect safety. She said that my little Sophie talked of me all day, and that I should find my son much improved on my return. I asked M. Rigerboos to give me his address, assuring him that at the proper time I should rely on his services.

A moment after Rigerboos had gone, I got a short note from Esther, who begged me, in her father's name, to spend the day with her—at least, if I had no important engagement. I answered that, excepting a certain matter of which her father knew, I had no chiefer aim than to convince her that I desired a place in her heart, and that she might be quite sure that I would not refuse her invitation.

I went to M. d'O—— at dinner time. I found Esther and her father puzzling over the method which drew reasonable answers out of a pyramid of numbers. As soon as her father saw me, he embraced me, saying how happy he was to possess a daughter capable of attracting me.

"She will attract any man who has sufficient sense to appreciate her."

"You appreciate her, then?"

"I worship her."

"Then embrace her."

Esther opened her arms, and with a cry of delight threw them round my neck, and gave the back all my caresses, kiss for kiss.

"I have got through all my business," said M. d'O——, "and the rest of my day is at your disposal. I have known from my childhood that there is such a science as the one you profess, and I was acquainted with a Jew who by its aid made an immense fortune. He, like you, said that, under pain of losing the secret, it could only be communicated to one person, but he put off doing so so long that at last it was too late, for a high fever carried him off in a few days. I hope you will not do as the Jew did; but in the meanwhile allow me to say that if You do not draw a profit from this treasure, you do not know what it really is."

"You call this knowledge of mine a treasure, and yet you possess one far more excellent," looking at Esther as I spoke.

"We will discuss that again. Yes, sir, I call your science a treasure."

"But the answers of the oracle are often very obscure."

"Obscure! The answers my daughter received are as clear as day."

"Apparently, she is fortunate in the way she frames her questions; for on this the reply depends."

"After dinner we will try if I am so fortunate—at least, if you will be so kind as to help me."

"I can refuse you nothing, as I consider father and daughter as one being."

At table we discussed other subjects, as the chief clerks were present—notably the manager, a vulgar-looking fellow, who had very evident aspirations in the direction of my fair Esther. After dinner we went into

M. d'O.'s private closet, and thereupon he drew two long questions out of his pocket. In the first he desired to know how to obtain a favourable decision from the States-General in an important matter, the details of which he explained. I replied in terms, the obscurity of which would have done credit to a professed Pythoness, and I left Esther to translate the answer into common sense, and find a meaning in it.

With regard to the second answer I acted in a different manner; I was impelled to answer clearly, and did so. M. d'O asked what had become of a vessel belonging to the India Company of which nothing had been heard. It was known to have started on the return voyage, and should have arrived two months ago, and this delay gave rise to the supposition that it had gone down. M. d'O—— wished to know if it were still above water, or whether it were lost, etc. As no tidings of it had come to hand, the company were on the look-out for someone to insure it, and offered ten per cent., but nobody cared to run so great a risk, especially as a letter had been received from an English sea captain who said he had seen her sink.

I may confess to my readers, though I did not do so to M. d'O——. that with inexplicable folly I composed an answer that left no doubt as to the safety of the vessel, pronouncing it safe and sound, and that we should hear of it in a few days. No doubt I felt the need of exalting my oracle, but this method was likely to destroy its credit for ever. In truth, if I had guessed M. d'O——'s design, I would have curbed my vanity, for I had no wish to make him lose a large sum without profiting myself.

The answer made him turn pale, and tremble with joy. He told us that secrecy in the matter was of the last importance, as he had determined to insure the vessel and drive a good bargain. At this, dreading the consequences, I hastened to tell him that for all I knew there might not be a word of truth in the oracle's reply, and that I should die of grief if I were the involuntary cause of his losing an enormous sum of money through relying on an oracle, the hidden sense of which might be completely opposed to the literal translation.

"Have you ever been deceived by it?"

"Often."

Seeing my distress, Esther begged her father to take no further steps in the matter. For some moments nobody spoke.

M. d'O—— looked thoughtful and full of the project which his fancy had painted in such gay colours. He said a good deal about it, dwelling on the mystic virtues of numbers, and told his daughter to read out all the questions she had addressed to the oracle with the answers she had received. There were six or seven of them, all briefly worded, some direct and some equivocal. Esther, who had constructed the pyramids, had shone, with my potent assistance, in extracting the answers, which I had really invented, and her father, in the joy of his heart, seeing her so clever, imagined that she would become an adept in the science by the force of intelligence. The lovely Esther, who was much taken with the trifle; was quite ready to be of the same opinion.

After passing several hours in the discussion of the answers, which my host thought divine, we had supper, and at parting M. d'O—— said that as Sunday was a day for pleasure and not business he hoped I would honour them by passing the day at their pretty house on the Amstel, and they were delighted at my accepting their invitation.

I could not help pondering over the mysteries of the commercial mind, which narrows itself down to considerations of profit and loss. M. d'O—— was decidedly an honest man; but although he was rich, he was by no means devoid of the greed incident to his profession. I asked myself the question, how a man, who would consider it dishonourable to steal a ducat, or to pick one up in the street and keep it, knowing to whom it belonged, could reconcile it with his conscience to make an enormous profit by insuring a vessel of the safety of which he was perfectly certain, as he believed the oracle infallible. Such a transaction was certainly fraudulent, as it is dishonest to play when one is certain of winning.

As I was going home I passed a tea-garden, and seeing a good many people going in and coming out I went in curious to know how these places were managed in Holland. Great heavens! I found myself the witness of an orgy, the scene a sort of cellar, a perfect cesspool of vice and debauchery. The discordant noise of the two or three instruments which formed the orchestra struck gloom to the soul and added to the horrors of the cavern. The air was dense with the fumes of bad tobacco, and vapours reeking of beer and garlic issued from every mouth. The company consisted of sailors, men of the lowest-class, and a number of vile women. The sailors and the dregs of the people thought this den a garden of delight, and considered its pleasures compensation for the toils of the sea and the miseries of daily labour. There was not a single woman there whose aspect had anything redeeming about it. I was looking at the repulsive sight in silence, when a great hulking fellow, whose appearance suggested the blacksmith, and his voice the blackguard, came up to me and asked me in bad Italian if I would like to dance. I answered in the negative, but before leaving me he pointed out a Venetian woman who, he said, would oblige me if I gave her some drink.

Wishing to discover if she was anyone I knew I looked at her attentively, and seemed to recollect her features, although I could not decide who she could be. Feeling rather curious on the subject I sat down next to her, and asked if she came from Venice, and if she had left that country some time ago.

"Nearly eighteen years," she replied.

I ordered a bottle of wine, and asked if she would take any; she said yes, and added, if I liked, she would oblige me.

"I haven't time," I said; and I gave the poor wretch the change I received from the waiter. She was full of gratitude, and would have embraced me if I had allowed her.

"Do you like being at Amsterdam better than Venice?" I asked.

"Alas, no! for if I were in my own country I should not be following this dreadful trade."

"How old were you when you left Venice."

"I was only fourteen and lived happily with my father and mother, who now may have died of grief."

"Who seduced you?"

"A rascally footman."

"In what part of Venice did you live?"

"I did not live in Venice, but at Friuli, not far off."

Friuli... eighteen years ago... a footman... I felt moved, and looking at the wretched woman more closely I soon recognized in her Lucie of Pasean. I cannot describe my sorrow, which I concealed as best I could, and tried hard to keep up my indifferent air. A life of debauchery rather than the flight of time had tarnished her beauty, and ruined the once exquisite outlines of her form. Lucie, that innocent and pretty maiden, grown ugly, vile, a common prostitute! It was a dreadful thought. She drank like a sailor, without looking at me, and without caring who I was. I took a few ducats from my purse, and slipped them into her hand, and without waiting for her to find out how much I had given her I left that horrible den.

I went to bed full of saddening thoughts. Not even under the Leads did I pass so wretched a day. I thought I must have risen under some unhappy star! I loathed myself. With regard to Lucie I felt the sting of remorse, but at the thought of M. d'O—— I hated myself. I considered that I should cause him a loss of three or four hundred thousand florins; and the thought was a bitter drop in the cup of my affection for Esther. I fancied, she, as well as her father, would become my implacable foe; and love that is not returned is no love at all.

I spent a dreadful night. Lucie, Esther, her father, their hatred of me, and my hatred of myself, were the groundwork of my dreams. I saw Esther and her father, if not ruined, at all events impoverished by my fault, and Lucie only thirty-two years old, and already deep in the abyss of vice, with an infinite prospect of misery and shame before her. The dawn was welcome indeed, for with its appearance a calm came to my spirit; it is, the darkness which is terrible to a heart full of remorse.

I got up and dressed myself in my best, and went in a coach to do my suit to the Princesse de Galitzin, who, was staying at the "Etoile d'Orient." I found her out; she had gone to the Admiralty. I went there, and found her accompanied by M. de Reissak and the Count de Tot, who had just received news of my friend Pesselier, at whose house I made his acquaintance, and who was dangerously ill when I left Paris.

I sent away my coach and began to walk towards M. d'O——'s house on the Amsel. The extreme elegance of my costume was displeasing in the eyes of the Dutch populace, and they hissed and hooted me, after the manner of the mob all the world over, Esther saw me coming from the window, drew the rope, and opened the door. I ran in, shut the door behind me, and as I was going up the wooden staircase, on the fourth or fifth step my foot struck against some yielding substance. I looked down and saw a green pocket-book. I stooped down to pick it up, but was awkward enough to send it through an opening in the stairs, which had been doubtless made for the purpose of giving light to a stair below. I did not stop, but went up the steps and was received with the usual hospitality, and on their expressing some wonder as to the unusual brilliance of my attire I explained the circumstances of the case. Esther smiled and said I looked quite another person, but I saw that both father and daughter were sad at heart. Esther's governess came in and said something to her in Dutch, at which, in evident distress, she ran and embraced her father.

"I see, my friends, that something has happened to you. If my presence is a restraint, treat me without ceremony, and bid me go."

"It's not so great an ill-hap after all; I have enough money left to bear the loss patiently."

"If I may ask the question, what is the nature of your loss?"

"I have lost a green pocket-book containing a good deal of money, which if I had been wise I would have left behind, as I did not require it till to-morrow."

"And you don't know where you lost it?"

"It must have been in the street, but I can't imagine how it can have happened. It contained bills of exchange for large amounts, and of course they don't matter, as I can stop payment of them, but there were also notes of the Bank of England for heavy sums, and they are gone, as they are payable to the bearer. Let us give thanks to God, my dear child, that it is no worse, and pray to Him to preserve to us what remains, and above all to keep us in good health. I have had much heavier losses than this, and I have been enabled not only to bear the misfortune but to make up the loss. Let us say no more about the matter."

While he was speaking my heart was full of joy, but I kept up the sadness befitting the scene. I had not the slightest doubt that the pocket-book in question was the one I had unluckily sent through the staircase, but which could not be lost irretrievably. My first point was how to make capital of my grand discovery in the interests of my cabalistic science. It was too fine an opportunity to be lost, especially as I still felt the sting of having been the cause of an enormous loss to the worthy man. I would give them a grand proof of the infallibility of my oracle: how many miracles are done in the same way! The thought put me into a good humour. I began to crack jokes, and my jests drew peals of laughter from Esther.

We had an excellent dinner and choice wine. After we had taken coffee I said that if they liked we would have a game of cards, but Esther said that this would be a waste of time, as she would much prefer making the oracular pyramids. This was exactly what I wanted.

"With all my heart," I said.

"We will do as you suggest."

"Shall I ask where my father lost his pocket-book?"

"Why not? It's a plain question: write it down."

She made the pyramid, and the reply was that the pocket-book had not been found by anyone. She leapt up from her seat, danced for joy, and threw her arms round her father's neck, saying,

"We shall find it, we shall find it, papa!"

"I hope so, too, my dear, that answer is really very consoling."

Wherewith Esther gave her father one kiss after another.

"Yes," said I, "there is certainly ground for hope, but the oracle will be dumb to all questions."

"Dumb! Why?"

"I was going to say it will be dumb if you do not give me as many kisses as you have given your father."

"Oh, then I will soon make it speak!" said she, laughing; and throwing her arms about my neck she began to kiss me, and I to give her kisses in return.

Ah! what happy days they seem when I recall them; and still I like dwelling on these days despite my sad old age, the foe of love. When I recall these events I grow young again and feel once more the delights of youth, despite the long years which separate me from that happy time.

At last Esther sat down again, and asked, "Where is the pocket-book?" And the pyramid told her that the pocket-book had fallen through the opening in the fifth step of the staircase.

M. d'O—— said to his daughter,

"Come, my dear Esther, let us go and test the truth of the oracle." And full of joy and hope they went to the staircase, I following them, and M. d'O shewed her the hole through which the pocket-book must have fallen. He lighted a candle and we went down to the cellar, and before long he picked up the book, which had fallen into some water. We went up again in high spirits, and there we talked for over an hour as seriously as you please on the divine powers of the oracle, which, according to them, should render its possessor the happiest of mortals.

He opened the pocket-book and shewed us the four thousand pound notes. He gave two to his daughter, and made me take the two remaining; but I took them with one hand and with the other gave them to Esther begging her to keep them for me; but before she would agree to do so I had to threaten her with the stoppage of the famous cabalistic oracle. I told M. d'O that all I asked was his friendship, and thereon he embraced me, and swore to be my friend to the death.

By making the fair Esther the depositary of my two thousand pounds, I was sure of winning her affection by an appeal, not to her interest, but to her truthfulness. This charming girl had about her so powerful an attraction that I felt as if my life was wound up with hers.

I told M. d'O that my chief object was to negotiate the twenty millions at a small loss.

"I hope to be of service to you in the matter," he said, "but as I. shall often want to speak to you, you must come and live in our house, which you must look upon as your own."

"My presence will be a restraint on you. I shall be a trouble."

"Ask Esther."

Esther joined her entreaties to her father's and I gave in, taking good care not to let them see how pleased I was. I contented myself with expressing my gratitude, to which they answered that it was I who conferred a favour.

M. d'O went into his closet, and as soon as I found myself alone with Esther I kissed her tenderly, saying that I should not be happy till I had won her heart.

"Do you love me?"

"Dearly, and I will do all in my power to shew how well I love you, if you will love me in return."

She gave me her hand, which I covered with kisses, and she went on to say, "As soon as you come and live with us, you must look out for a good opportunity for asking my hand of my father. You need not be afraid he will refuse you, but the first thing for you to do is to move into our house."

"My dear little wife! I will come to-morrow."

We said many sweet things to one another, talked about the future, and told each other our inmost thoughts; and I was undoubtedly truly in love, for not a single improper fancy rose in my mind in the presence of my dear who loved me so well.

The first thing that M. d'O said on his return was, that there would be a piece of news on the Exchange the next day.

"What is that, papa dear?"

"I have decided to take the whole risk—amounting to three hundred thousand florins-of the ship which is thought to have gone down. They will call me mad, but they themselves will be the madmen; which is what I should be if, after the proof we have had, I doubted the oracle any more."

"My dear sir, you make me frightened. I have told you that I have been often deceived by the oracle."

"That must have been, my dear fellow, when the reply was obscure, and you did not get at the real sense of it; but in the present case there is no room, for doubt. I shall make three million florins, or, if the worst comes to the worse, my loss won't ruin me."

Esther, whom the finding of the pocket-book had made enthusiastic, told her father to lose no time. As for me, I could not recall what I had done, but I was again overwhelmed with sadness. M. d'O—— saw it, and taking my hand said, "If the oracle does lie this time, I shall be none the less your friend."

"I am glad to hear it," I answered; "but as this is a matter of the utmost importance, let me consult the oracle a second time before you risk your three hundred thousand florins." This proposition pleased the father and daughter highly; they could not express their gratitude to me for being so careful of their interests.

What followed was truly surprising—enough to make one believe in fatality. My readers probably will not believe it; but as these Memoirs will not be published till I have left this world, it would be of no use for me to disguise the truth in any way, especially as the writing of them is only the amusement of my leisure hours. Well, let him who will believe it; this is absolutely what happened. I wrote down the question myself, erected the pyramid, and carried out all the magical ceremonies without letting Esther have a hand in it. I was delighted to be able to check an act of extreme imprudence, and I was determined to do so. A double meaning, which I knew how to get, would abate M. d'O——'s courage and annihilate his plans. I had thought over what I wanted to say, and I thought I had expressed it properly in the numbers. With that idea, as Esther knew the alphabet perfectly well, I let her extract the answer, and transfer it into letters. What was my surprise when I heard her read these words:

"In a matter of this kind neither fear nor hesitate. Your repentance would be too hard for you to bear."

That was enough. Father and daughter ran to embrace me, and M. d'O-said that when the vessel was sighted a tithe of the profits should be mine. My surprise prevented me giving any answer; I had intended to write trust and hazard, and I had written fear and hesitate. But thanks to his prejudice, M. d'O—— only saw in my silence confirmation of the infallibility of the oracle. In short, I could do nothing more, and I took my leave leaving everything to the care of chance, who sometimes is kind to us in spite of ourselves.

The next morning I took up my abode in a splendid suite of rooms in Esther's house, and the day after I took her to a concert, where she joked with me on the grief I should endure on account of the absence of Madame Trend and my daughter. Esther was the only mistress of my soul. I lived but to adore her, and I should have satisfied my love had not Esther been a girl of good principles. I could not gain possession of her, and was full of longing and desire.

Four or five days after my installation in my new quarters, M. d'O——communicated to me the result of a conference which he had had with M. Pels and six other bankers on the twenty millions. They offered ten millions in hard cash and seven millions in paper money, bearing interest at five or six per cent. with a deduction of one per cent. brokerage. Furthermore, they would forgive a sum of twelve hundred thousand florins owed by the French India Company to the Dutch Company.

With such conditions I could not venture to decide on my own responsibility, although, personally, I thought them reasonable enough, the impoverished state of the French treasury being taken into consideration. I sent copies of the proposal to M. de Boulogne and M. d'Afri, begging from them an immediate reply. At the end of a week I received an answer in the writing of M. de Courteil, acting for M. de Boulogne, instructing me to refuse absolutely any such proposal, and to report myself at Paris if I saw no chance of making a better bargain. I was again informed that peace was imminent, though the Dutch were quite of another opinion.

In all probability I should have immediately left for Paris, but for a circumstance which astonished nobody but myself in the family of which I had become a member. The confidence of M. d'O—— increased every day, and as if chance was determined to make me a prophet in spite of myself, news was received of the ship which was believed to be lost, and which, on the faith of my oracle, M. d'O had bought for three hundred thousand florins. The vessel was at Madeira. The joy of Esther, and still more my own, may be imagined when we saw the worthy man enter the house triumphantly with confirmation of the good news.

"I have insured the vessel from Madeira to the mouth of the Texel for a trifle," said he, "and so," turning to me, "you may count from this moment on the tenth part of the profit, which I owe entirely to you."

The reader may imagine my delight; but there is one thing he will not imagine, unless he knows my character better than I do myself, the confusion into which I was thrown by the following remarks:

"You are now rich enough," said M. d'O——, "to set up for yourself amongst us, and you are positively certain to make an enormous fortune in a short time merely by making use of your cabala. I will be your agent; let us live together, and if you like my daughter as she likes you, you can call yourself my son as soon as you please."

In Esther's face shone forth joy and happiness, and in mine, though I adored her, there was to be seen, alas! nothing but surprise. I was stupid with happiness and the constraint in which I held myself. I did not analyze my feelings, but, though I knew it not, there can be no doubt that my insuperable objection to the marriage tie was working within my soul. A long silence followed; and last, recovering my powers of speech, I succeeded, with an effort, in speaking to them of my gratitude, my happiness, my love, and I ended by saying that, in spite of my affection for Esther, I must, before settling in Holland, return to Paris, and discharge the confidential and responsible duty which the Government had placed in my hands. I would then return to Amsterdam perfectly independent.

This long peroration won their approval. Esther was quite pleased, and we spent the rest of the day in good spirits. Next day M. d'O—— gave a splendid dinner to several of his friends, who congratulated him on his good fortune, being persuaded that his courageous action was to be explained by his having had secret information of the safety of the vessel, though none of them could see from what source he, and he only, had obtained it.

A week after this lucky event he gave me an ultimatum on the matter of the twenty millions, in which he guaranteed that France should not lose more than nine per cent. in the transaction.

I immediately sent a copy of his proposal to M. d'Afri, begging him to be as prompt as possible, and another copy to the comptroller-general, with a letter in which I warned him that the thing would certainly fall through if he delayed a single day in sending full powers to M. d'Afri to give me the necessary authority to act.

I wrote to the same effect to M. de Courteil and the Duc de Choiseul, telling them that I was to receive no brokerage; but that I should all the same accept a proposal which I thought a profitable one, and saying that I had no doubt of obtaining my expenses from the French Government.

As it was a time of rejoicing with us, M. d'O—— thought it would be a good plan to give a ball. All the most distinguished people in Amsterdam were invited to it. The ball and supper were of the most splendid description, and Esther, who was a blaze of diamonds, danced all the quadrilles with me, and charmed every beholder by her grace and beauty.

I spent all my time with Esther, and every day we grew more and more in love, and more unhappy, for we were tormented by abstinence, which irritated while it increased our desires.

Esther was an affectionate mistress, but discreet rather by training than disposition the favours she accorded me were of the most insignificant description. She was lavish of nothing but her kisses, but kisses are rather irritating than soothing. I used to be nearly wild with love. She told me, like other virtuous women, that if she agreed to make me happy she was sure I would not marry her, and that as soon as I made her my wife she would be mine and mine only. She did not think I was married, for I had given her too many assurances to the contrary, but she thought I had a strong attachment to someone in Paris. I confessed that she was right, and said that I was going there to put an end to it that I might be bound to her alone. Alas! I lied when I said so, for Esther was inseparable from her father, a man of forty, and I could not make up my mind to pass the remainder of my days in Holland.

Ten or twelve days after sending the ultimatum, I received a letter from M. de Boulogne informing me that M. d'Afri had all necessary instructions for effecting the exchange of the twenty millions, and another letter from the ambassador was to the same effect. He warned me to take care that everything was right, as he should not part with the securities before receiving 18,200,000 francs in current money.

The sad time of parting at last drew near, amid many regrets and tears from all of us. Esther gave me the two thousand pounds I had won so easily, and her father at my request gave me bills of exchange to the amount of a hundred thousand florins, with a note of two hundred thousand florins authorizing me to draw upon him till the whole sum was exhausted. Just as I was going, Esther gave me fifty shirts and fifty handkerchiefs of the finest quality.

It was not my love for Manon Baletti, but a foolish vanity and a desire to cut a figure in the luxurious city of Paris, which made me leave Holland. But such was the disposition that Mother Nature had given me that fifteen months under The Leads had not been enough to cure this mental malady of mine. But when I reflect upon after events of my life I am not astonished that The Leads proved ineffectual, for the numberless vicissitudes which I have gone through since have not cured me—my disorder, indeed, being of the incurable kind. There is no such thing as destiny. We ourselves shape our lives, notwithstanding that saying of the Stoics, 'Volentem ducit, nolentem trahit'.

After promising Esther to return before the end of the year, I set out with a clerk of the company who had brought the French securities, and I reached the Hague, where Boaz received me with a mingled air of wonder and admiration. He told me that I had worked a miracle; "but," he added, "to succeed thus you must have persuaded them that peace was on the point of being concluded."

"By no means," I answered; "so far from my persuading them, they are of the opposite opinion; but all the same I may tell you that peace is really imminent."

"If you like to give me that assurance in writing," said he, "I will make you a present of fifty thousand florins' worth of diamonds."

"Well," I answered, "the French ambassador is of the same opinion as myself; but I don't think the certainty is sufficiently great as yet for you to risk your diamonds upon it."

Next day I finished my business with the ambassador, and the clerk returned to Amsterdam.

I went to supper at Therese's, and found her children very well dressed. I told her to go on to Rotterdam the next day and wait for me there with her son, as I had no wish to give scandal at the Hague.

At Rotterdam, Therese told me that she knew I had won half a million at Amsterdam, and that her fortune would be made if she could leave Holland for London. She had instructed Sophie to tell me that my good luck was the effect of the prayers she had addressed to Heaven on my behalf. I saw where the land lay, and I enjoyed a good laugh at the mother's craft and the child's piety, and gave her a hundred ducats, telling her that she should have another hundred when she wrote to me from London. It was very evident that she thought the sum a very moderate one, but I would not give her any more. She waited for the moment when I was getting into my carriage to beg me to give her another hundred ducats, and I said, in a low tone, that she should have a thousand if she would give me her daughter. She thought it over for a minute, and then said that she could not part with her.

"I know very well why," I answered; and drawing a watch from my fob I gave it to Sophie, embraced her, and went on my way. I arrived at Paris on February 10th, and took sumptuous apartments near the Rue Montorgueil.

II

I Meet with a Flattering Reception from My Patron—
Madame D'Urfe's Infatuation—Madame X. C. V. and
her Family—Madame du Rumain

During my journey from the Hague to Paris, short as it was, I had plenty of opportunities for seeing that the mental qualities of my adopted son were by no means equal to his physical ones.

As I had said, the chief point which his mother had impressed on him was reserve, which she had instilled into him out of regard for her own interests. My readers will understand what I mean, but the child, in following his mother's instructions, had gone beyond the bounds of moderation; he possessed reserve, it is true, but he was also full of dissimulation, suspicion, and hypocrisy—a fine trio of deceit in one who was still a boy. He not only concealed what he knew, but he pretended to know that which he did not. His idea of the one quality necessary to success in life was an impenetrable reserve, and to obtain this he had accustomed himself to silence the dictates of his heart, and to say no word that had not been carefully weighed. Giving other people wrong impressions passed with him for discretion, and his soul being incapable of a generous thought, he seemed likely to pass through life without knowing what friendship meant.

Knowing that Madame d'Urfe counted on the boy for the accomplishment of her absurd hypostasis, and that the more mystery I made of his birth the more extravagant would be her fancies about it, I told the lad that if I introduced him to a lady who questioned him by himself about his birth, he was to be perfectly open with her.

On my arrival at Paris my first visit was to my patron, whom I found in grand company amongst whom I recognized the Venetian ambassador, who pretended not to know me.

"How long have you been in Paris?" said the minister, taking me by the hand.

"I have only just stepped out of my chaise."

"Then go to Versailles. You will find the Duc de Choiseul and the comptroller-general there. You have been wonderfully successful, go and get your meed of praise and come and see me afterwards. Tell the duke that Voltaire's appointment to be a gentleman-in-ordinary to the king is ready."

I was not going to start for Versailles at midday, but ministers in Paris are always talking in this style, as if Versailles were at the end of the street. Instead of going there, I went to see Madame d'Urfe.

She received me with the words that her genius had informed her that I should come to-day, and that she was delighted with the fulfilment of the prophecy.

"Corneman tells me that you have been doing wonders in Holland; but I see more in the matter than he does, as I am quite certain that you have taken over the twenty millions yourself. The funds have risen, and a hundred millions at least will be in circulation in the course of the next week. You must not be offended at my shabby present, for, of course, twelve thousand francs are nothing to you. You must look upon them as a little token of friendship."

"I am going to tell my servants to close all the doors, for I am too glad to see you not to want to have you all to myself."

A profound bow was the only reply I made to this flattering speech, and I saw her tremble with joy when I told her that I had brought a lad of twelve with me, whom I intended to place in the best school I could find that he might have a good education.

"I will send him myself to Viar, where my nephews are. What is his name? Where is he? I know well what this boy is, I long to see him. Why did you not alight from your journey at my house?"

Her questions and replies followed one another in rapid succession. I should have found it impossible to get in a word edgeways, even if I had wanted to, but I was very glad to let her expend her enthusiasm, and took good care not to interrupt her. On the first opportunity, I told her that I should have the pleasure of presenting the young gentleman to her the day after tomorrow, as on the morrow I had an engagement at Versailles.

"Does the dear lad speak French? While I am arranging for his going to school you must really let him come and live with me."

"We will discuss that question on the day after tomorrow, madam."

"Oh, how I wish the day after to-morrow was here!"

On leaving Madame d'Urfe I went to my lottery office and found everything in perfect order. I then went to the Italian play, and found Silvia and her daughter in their dressing-room.

"My dear friend," said she when she saw me, "I know that you have achieved a wonderful success in Holland, and I congratulate you."

I gave her an agreeable surprise by saying that I had been working for her daughter, and Marion herself blushed, and lowered her eyes in a very suggestive manner. "I will be with you at supper," I added, "and then we can talk at our ease." On leaving them I went to the amphitheatre, and what was my surprise to see in one of the first boxes Madame X—— C—— V——, with all her family. My readers will be glad to hear their history.

Madame X—— C—— V——, by birth a Greek, was the widow of an Englishman, by whom she had six children, four of whom were girls. On his death-bed he became a Catholic out of deference to the tears of his wife; but as his children could not inherit his forty thousand pounds invested in England, without conforming to the Church of England, the family returned to London, where the widow complied with all the obligations of the law of England. What will people not do when their interests are at stake! though in a case like this there is no need to blame a person for yielding, to prejudices which had the sanction of the law.

It was now the beginning of the year 1758, and five years before, when I was at Padua, I fell in love with the eldest daughter, but a few months after, when we were at Venice, Madame X. C. V. thought good to exclude me from her family circle. The insult which the mother put upon me was softened by the daughter, who wrote me a charming letter, which I love to read even now. I may as well confess that my grief was the easier to bear as my time was taken up by my fair nun, M—— M——, and my dear C—— C——. Nevertheless, Mdlle. X. C. V., though only fifteen, was of a perfect beauty, and was all the more charming in that to her physical advantages she joined those of a cultured mind.

Count Algarotti, the King of Prussia's chamberlain, gave her lessons, and several young nobles were among her suitors, her preference apparently being given to the heir of the family of Memmo de St. Marcuola. He died a year afterwards, while he was procurator.

My surprise at seeing this family at such a time and place may be imagined. Mdlle. X. C. V. saw me directly, and pointed me out to her mother, who made a sign to me with her fan to come to their box.

She received me in the friendliest manner possible, telling me that we were not at Venice now, and that she hoped I would often come and see them at the "Hotel de Bretagne," in the Rue St. Andre des Arts. I told them that I did not wish to recall any events which might have happened at Venice, and her daughter having joined her entreaties to those of her mother, I promised to accept their invitation.

Mdlle. X. C. V. struck me as prettier than ever; and my love, after sleeping for five years, awoke to fresh strength and vigour. They told me that they were going to pass six months at Paris before returning to Venice. In return I informed them that I intended making Paris my home, that I had just left Holland, that I was going to Versailles the next day, so that I could not pay my respects to them till the day after. I also begged them to accept my services, in a manner which let them know I was a person of some importance.

Mdlle. X. C. V. said that she was aware that the results of my Dutch mission should render me dear to France, that she had always lived in hopes of seeing me once more, that my famous flight from The Leads had delighted them; "for," she added, "we have always been fond of you."

"I fancy your mother has kept her fondness for me very much to herself," I whispered to her.

"We won't say anything about that," said she in the same tone. "We learnt all the circumstances of your wonderful flight from a letter of sixteen pages you wrote to M. Memmo. We trembled with joy and shuddered with fear as we read it."

"How did you know I have been in Holland?"

"M. de la Popeliniere told us about it yesterday."

M. de la Popeliniere, the fermier-general, whom I had known seven years ago at Passi, came into the box just as his name was spoken. After complimenting me he said that if I could carry through the same operation for the India Company my fortune would be made.

"My advice to you is," he said, "to get yourself naturalized before it becomes generally known that you have made half a million of money."

"Half a million! I only wish I had!"

"You must have made that at the lowest calculation."

"On the contrary, I give you my assurance, that if my claim for brokerage is not allowed, the transaction will prove absolutely ruinous to me."

"Ah! no doubt you are right to take that tone. Meanwhile, everyone wants to make your acquaintance, for France is deeply indebted to you. You have caused the funds to recover in a very marked degree."

After the play was over I went to Silvia's, where I was received as if I had been the favourite child of the family; but on the other hand I gave them certain proofs that I wished to be regarded in that light. I was impressed with the idea that to their unshaken friendship I owed all my good luck, and I made the father, mother, the daughter, and the two sons, receive the presents I had got for them. The best was for the mother, who handed it on to her daughter. It was a pair of diamond ear-rings of great beauty, for which I had given fifteen thousand francs. Three days after I sent her a box containing fine linen from Holland, and choice Mechlin and Alencon lace. Mario, who liked smoking, got a gold pipe; the father a choice gold and enamelled snuff-box, and I gave a repeater to the younger son, of whom I was very fond. I shall have occasion later on to speak of this lad, whose natural qualities were far superior to his position in life. But, you will ask, was I rich enough to make such presents? No, I was not, and I knew it perfectly well; but I gave these presents because I was afraid of not being able to do so if I waited.

I set out for Versailles at day-break, and M. de Choiseul received me as before, his hair was being dressed, but for a moment he laid down his pen, which shewed that I had become a person of greater importance in his eyes. After a slight but grateful compliment, he told me that if I thought myself capable of negotiating a loan of a hundred millions to bear interest at four per cent., he would do all in his power to help me. My answer was that I would think it over when I heard how much I was to have for what I had done already.

"But everybody says that you have made two hundred thousand florins by it."

"That would not be so bad; half a million of francs would be a fair foundation on which to build a fortune; but I can assure your excellence that there is not a word of truth in the report. I defy anyone to prove it; and till some substantial proof is offered, I think I can lay claim to brokerage."

"True, true. Go to the comptroller-general and state your views to him."

M. de Boulogne stopped the occupation on which he was engaged to give me a most friendly greeting, but when I said that he owed me a hundred thousand florins he smiled sardonically.

"I happen to know," he said, "that you have bills of exchange to the amount of a hundred thousand crowns payable to yourself."

"Certainly, but that money has no connection with my mission, as I can prove to you by referring you to M. d'Afri. I have in my head an infallible project for increasing the revenue by twenty millions, in a manner which will cause no irritation."

"You don't say so! Communicate your plan, and I promise to get you a pension of a hundred thousand francs, and letters of nobility as well, if you like to become a Frenchman."

"I will think it over."

On leaving M. de Boulogne I went to the Palace, where a ballet was going on before the Marquise de Pompadour.

She bowed to me as soon as she saw me, and on my approaching her she told me that I was an able financier, and that the "gentlemen below" could not appreciate my merits. She had not forgotten what I had said to her eight years before in the theatre at Fontainebleau. I replied that all good gifts were from above, whither, with her help, I hoped to attain.

On my return to Paris I went to the "Hotel Bourbon" to inform my patron of the result of my journey. His advice to me was to continue to serve the Government well, as its good fortune would come to be mine. On my telling him of my meeting with the X. C. V. 's, he said that M. de la Popeliniere was going to marry the elder daughter.

When I got to my house my son was nowhere to be found. My landlady told me that a great lady had come to call on my lord, and that she had taken him away with her. Guessing that this was Madame d'Urfe, I went to bed without troubling myself any further. Early next morning my clerk brought me a letter. It came from the old attorney, uncle to Gaetan's wife, whom I had helped to escape from the jealous fury of her brutal husband. The attorney begged me to come and speak to him at the courts, or to make an appointment at some place where he could see me. I went to the courts and found him there.

"My niece," he began, "found herself obliged to go into a convent; and from this vantage ground she is pleading against her husband, with the aid of a barrister, who will be responsible for the costs. However, to win our case, we require the evidence of yourself, Count Tiretta, and other servants who witnessed the scene at the inn."

I did all I could, and four months afterwards Gaetan simplified matters by a fraudulent bankruptcy, which obliged him to leave France: in due time and place, I shall have something more to say about him. As for his wife, who was young and pretty, she paid her counsel in love's money, and was very happy with him, and may be happy still for all I know, but I have entirely lost sight of her.

After my interview with the old attorney I went to Madame—— to see Tiretta, who was out. Madame was still in love with him, and he continued to make a virtue of necessity. I left my address, and went to the "Hotel de Bretagne" to pay my first call on Madame X. C. V. The lady, though she was not over fond of me, received me with great politeness. I possibly cut a better figure in her eyes when rich, and at Paris, then when we were in Venice. We all know that diamonds have the strange power of fascination, and that they form an excellent substitute for virtue!

Madame X. C. V. had with her an old Greek named Zandiri, brother to M. de Bragadin's major-domo, who was just dead. I uttered some expressions of sympathy, and the boor did not take the trouble to answer me, but I was avenged for his foolish stiffness by the enthusiasm with which I was welcomed by everyone else. The eldest girl, her sisters, and the two sons, almost overwhelmed me with friendliness. The eldest son was only fourteen, and was a young fellow of charming manners, but evidently extremely independent, and sighed for the time when he would be able to devote himself to a career of profligacy for which he was well fitted. Mdlle. X. C. V. was both beautiful and charming in her manner, and had received an excellent education of which, however, she made no parade. One could not stay in her presence without loving her, but she was no flirt, and I soon saw that she held out no vain hopes to those who had the misfortune not to please her. Without being rude she knew how to be cold, and it was all the worse for those whom her coldness did not shew that their quest was useless.

The first hour I passed in her company chained me a captive to her triumphant car. I told her as much, and she replied that she was glad to have such a captive. She took the place in my heart where Esther had reigned a week before, but I freely confess that Esther yielded only because she was away. As to my attachment to Sylvia's daughter, it was of such a nature as not to hinder me falling in love with any other woman who chanced to take my fancy. In the libertine's heart love cannot exist without substantial food, and women who have had some experience of the world are well aware of this fact. The youthful Baletti was a beginner, and so knew nothing of these things.

M. Farsetti, a Venetian of noble birth, a knight of Malta, a great student of the occult sciences, and a good Latin versifier, came in at one o'clock. Dinner was just ready and Madame X. C. V. begged him to stay. She asked me also to dine with them, but wishing to dine with Madame d'Urfe I refused the invitation for the nonce.

M. Farsetti, who had known me very well at Venice, only noticed me by a side-glance, and without shewing any vexation I paid him back in the same coin. He smiled at Mdlle. X. C. V. 's praise of my courage. She noticed his expression, and as if to punish him for it went on to say that I had now the admiration of every Venetian, and that the French were anxious to have the honour of calling me a fellow-citizen. M. Farsetti asked me if my post at the lottery paid well. I replied, coolly,

"Oh, yes, well enough for me to pay my clerks' salaries."

He understood the drift of my reply, and Mdlle. X. C. V. smiled.

I found my supposed son with Madame d'Urfe, or rather in that amiable visionary's arms. She hastened to apologize for carrying him off, and I turned it off with a jest, having no other course to take.

"I made him sleep with me," she said, "but I shall be obliged to deprive myself of this privilege for the future, unless he promises to be more discreet."

I thought the idea a grand one, and the little fellow, in spite of his blushes, begged her to say how he had offended.

"We shall have the Comte de St. Germain," said Madame d'Urfe, "to dinner. I know he amuses you, and I like you to enjoy yourself in my house."

"For that, madam, your presence is all I need; nevertheless, I thank you for considering me."

In due course St. Germain arrived, and in his usual manner sat himself down, not to eat but to talk. With a face of imperturbable gravity he told the most incredible stories, which one had to pretend to believe, as he was always either the hero of the tale or an eye witness of the event. All the same, I could not help bursting into laughter when he told us of something that happened as he was dining with the Fathers of the Council of Trent.

Madame d'Urfe wore on her neck a large magnet. She said that it would one day happen that this magnet would attract the lightning, and that she would consequently soar into the sun. I longed to tell her that when she got there she could be no higher up than on the earth, but I restrained myself; and the great charlatan hastened to say that there could be no doubt about it, and that he, and he only, could increase the force of the magnet a thousand times. I said, dryly, that I would wager twenty thousand crowns he would not so much as double its force, but Madame d'Urfe would not let us bet, and after dinner she told me in private that I should have lost, as St. Germain was a magician. Of course I agreed with her.

A few days later, the magician set out for Chambord, where the king had given him a suite of rooms and a hundred thousand francs, that he might be at liberty to work on the dyes which were to assure the superiority of French materials over those of any other country. St. Germain had got over the king by arranging a laboratory where he occasionally tried to amuse himself, though he knew little about chemistry, but the king was the victim of an almost universal weariness. To enjoy a harem recruited from amongst the most ravishing beauties, and often from the ranks of neophytes, with whom pleasure had its difficulties, one would have needed to be a god, and Louis XV was only a man after all.

It was the famous marquise who had introduced the adept to the king in the hope of his distracting the monarch's weariness, by giving him a taste for chemistry. Indeed Madame de Pompadour was under the impression that St. Germain had given her the water of perpetual youth, and therefore felt obliged to make the chemist a good return. This wondrous water, taken according to the charlatan's directions, could not indeed make old age retire and give way to youth, but according to the marquise it would preserve one in statu quo for several centuries.

As a matter of fact, the water, or the giver of it, had worked wonders, if not on her body, at least on her mind; she assured the king that she was not getting older. The king was as much deluded by this grand impostor as she was, for one day he shewed the Duc des Deux-Ponts a diamond of the first water, weighing twelve carats, which he fancied he had made himself. "I melted down," said Louis XV, "small diamonds weighing twenty-four carats, and obtained this one large one weighing twelve." Thus it came to pass that the infatuated monarch gave the impostor the suite formerly occupied by Marshal Saxe. The Duc des Deux-Ponts told me this story with his own lips, one evening, when I was supping with him and a Swede, the Comte de Levenhoop, at Metz.

Before I left Madame d'Urfe, I told her that the lad might be he who should make her to be born again, but that she would spoil all if she did not wait for him to attain the age of puberty. After what she had said about his misbehavior, the reader will guess what made me say this. She sent him to board with Viar, gave him masters on everything, and disguised him under the name of the Comte d'Aranda, although he was born at Bayreuth, and though his mother never had anything to do with a Spaniard of that name. It was three or four months before I went to see him, as I was afraid of being insulted on account of the name which the visionary Madame d'Urfe had given him.

One day Tiretta came to see me in a fine coach. He told me that his elderly mistress wanted to become his wife, but that he would not hear of it, though she offered to endow him with all her worldly goods. I told him that if he gave in he might pay his debts, return to Trevisa, and live pleasantly there; but his destiny would not allow him to take my advice.

I had resolved on taking a country house, and fixed on one called "Little Poland," which pleased me better than all the others I had seen. It was well furnished, and was a hundred paces distant from the Madeleine Gate. It was situated on slightly elevated ground near the royal park, behind the Duc de Grammont's garden, and its owner had given it the name of "Pleasant Warsaw." It had two gardens, one of which was on a level with the first floor, three reception rooms, large stables, coach houses, baths, a good cellar, and a splendid kitchen. The master was called "The Butter King," and always wrote himself down so; the name had been given to him by Louis XV on the monarch's stopping at the house and liking the butter. The "Butter King" let me his house for a hundred Louis per annum, and he gave me an excellent cook called "The Pearl," a true blue-ribbon of the order of cooks, and to her he gave charge of all his furniture and the plate I should want for a dinner of six persons, engaging to get me as much plate as I wanted at the hire of a sous an ounce. He also promised to let me have what wine I wanted, and said all he had was of the best, and, moreover, cheaper than I could get it at Paris, as he had no gate-money to pay on it.

Matters having been arranged on these terms, in the course of a week I got a good coachman, two fine carriages, five horses, a groom, and two footmen. Madame d'Urfe, who was my first guest, was delighted with my new abode, and as she imagined that I had done it all for her, I left her in that flattering opinion. I never could believe in the morality of snatching from poor mortal man the delusions which make them happy. I also let her retain the notion that young d'Aranda, the count of her own making, was a scion of the nobility, that he was born for a mysterious operation unknown to the rest of mankind, that I was only his caretaker (here I spoke the truth), and that he must die and yet not cease to live. All these whimsical ideas were the products of her brain, which was only occupied with the impossible, and I thought the best thing I could do was to agree with everything. If I had tried to undeceive her, she would have accused me of want of trust in her, for she was convinced that all her knowledge was revealed to her by her genius, who spoke to her only by night. After she had dined with me I took her back to her house, full of happiness.

GIACOMO CASANOVA

Camille sent me a lottery ticket, which she had invested in at my office, and which proved to be a winning one, I think, for a thousand crowns or thereabouts. She asked me to come and sup with her, and bring the money with me. I accepted her invitation, and found her surrounded by all the girls she knew and their lovers. After supper I was asked to go to the opera with them, but we had scarcely got there when I lost my party in the crowd. I had no mask on, and I soon found myself attacked by a black domino, whom I knew to be a woman, and as she told me a hundred truths about myself in a falsetto voice, I was interested, and determined on finding out who she was. At last I succeeded in persuading her to come with me into a box, and as soon as we were in and I had taken off her mask I was astonished to find she was Mdlle. X. C. V.

"I have come to the ball," said she, "with one of my sisters, my elder brother, and M. Farsetti. I left them to go into a box and change my domino:

"They must feel very uneasy."

"I dare say they do, but I am not going to take pity on them till the end of the ball."

Finding myself alone with her, and certain of having her in my company for the rest of the night, I began to talk of our old love-making; and I took care to say that I was more in love with her than ever. She listened to me kindly, did not oppose my embraces, and by the few obstacles she placed in my way I judged that the happy moment was not far off. Nevertheless I felt that I must practice restraint that evening, and she let me see that she was obliged to me.

"I heard at Versailles, my dear mademoiselle, that you are going to marry M. de la Popeliniere."

"So they say. My mother wishes me to do so, and the old financier fancies he has got me in his talons already; but he makes a mistake, as I will never consent to such a thing."

"He is old, but he is very rich."

"He is very rich and very generous, for he promises me a dowry of a million if I become a widow without children; and if I had a son he would leave me all his property."

"You wouldn't have much difficulty in complying with the second alternative."

"I shall never have anything to do with his money, for I should never make my life miserable by a marriage with a man whom I do not love, while I do love another."

"Another! Who is the fortunate mortal to whom you have given your heart's treasure?"

"I do not know if my loved one is fortunate. My lover is a Venetian, and my mother knows of it; but she says that I should not be happy, that he is not worthy of me."

"Your mother is a strange woman, always crossing your affections."

"I cannot be angry with her. She may possibly be wrong, but she certainly loves me. She would rather that I should marry M. Farsetti, who would be very glad to have me, but I detest him."

"Has he made a declaration in terms?"

"He has, and all the marks of contempt I have given him seem to have no effect."

"He clings hard to hope; but the truth is you have fascinated him."

"Possibly, but I do not think him susceptible of any tender or generous feeling. He is a visionary; surly, jealous, and envious in his disposition. When he heard me expressing myself about you in the manner you deserve, he had the impudence to say to my mother before my face that she ought not to receive you."

"He deserves that I should give him a lesson in manners, but there are other ways in which he may be punished. I shall be delighted to serve you in any way I can."

"Alas! if I could only count on your friendship I should be happy."

The sigh with which she uttered these words sent fire through my veins, and I told her that I was her devoted slave; that I had fifty thousand crowns which were at her service, and that I would risk my life to win her favours. She replied that she was truly grateful to me, and as she threw her arms about my neck our lips met, but I saw that she was weeping, so I took care that the fire which her kisses raised should be kept within bounds. She begged me to come and see her often, promising that as often as she could manage it we should be alone. I could ask no more, and after I had promised to come and dine with them on the morrow, we parted.

I passed an hour in walking behind her, enjoying my new position of intimate friend, and I then returned to my Little Poland. It was a short distance, for though I lived in the country I could get to any part of Paris in a quarter of an hour. I had a clever coachman, and capital horses not used to being spared. I got them from the royal stables, and as soon as I lost one I got another from the same place, having to pay two hundred francs. This happened to me several times, for, to my mind, going fast is one of the greatest pleasures which Paris offers.

Having accepted an invitation to dinner at the X. C. V.'s, I did not give myself much time for sleep, and I went out on foot with a cloak on. The snow was falling in large flakes, and when I got to madame's I was as white as a sheet from head to foot. She gave me a hearty welcome, laughing, and saying that her daughter had been telling her how she had puzzled me, and that she was delighted to see me come to dinner without ceremony. "But," added she, "it's Friday today, and you will have to fast, though, after all, the fish is very good. Dinner is not ready yet. You had better go and see my daughter, who is still a-bed."

As may be imagined, this invitation had not to be repeated, for a pretty woman looks better in bed than anywhere else. I found Mdlle. X. C. V. sitting up in bed writing, but she stopped as soon as she saw me.

"How is this, sweet lie-a-bed, not up yet?"

"Yes, I am staying in bed partly because I feel lazy, and partly because I am freer here."

"I was afraid you were not quite well."

"Nor am I. However, we will say no more about that now. I am just going to take some soup, as those who foolishly establish the institution of fasting were not polite enough to ask my opinion on the subject. It does not agree with my health, and I don't like it, so I am not going to get up even to sit at table, though I shall thus deprive myself of your society."

I naturally told her that in her absence dinner would have no savour; and I spoke the truth.

As the presence of her sister did not disturb us, she took out of her pocket-book an epistle in verse which I had addressed to her when her mother had forbidden me the house. "This fatal letter," said she, "which you called 'The Phoenix,' has shaped my life and may prove the cause of my death."

I had called it the Phoenix because, after bewailing my unhappy lot, I proceeded to predict how she would afterwards give her heart to a mortal whose qualities would make him deserve the name of Phoenix. A hundred lines were taken up in the description of these imaginary mental and moral characteristics, and certainly the being who should have them all would be right worthy of worship, for he would be rather a god than a man.

"Alas!" said Mdlle. X. C. V., "I fell in love with this imaginary being, and feeling certain that such an one must exist I set myself to look for him. After six months I thought I had found him. I gave him my heart, I received his, we loved each other fondly. But for the last four months we have been separated, and during the whole time I have only had one letter from him. Yet I must not blame him, for I know he cannot help it. Such, is my sorry fate: I can neither hear from him nor write to him:"

This story was a confirmation of a theory of mine namely, that the most important events in our lives proceed often from the most trifling causes. My epistle was nothing better than a number of lines of poetry more or less well written, and the being I had delineated was certainly not to be found, as he surpassed by far all human perfections, but a woman's heart travels so quickly and so far! Mdlle. X. C. V. took the thing literally, and fell in love with a chimera of goodness, and then was fain to turn this into a real lover, not thinking of the vast difference between the ideal and the real. For all that, when she thought that she had found the original of my fancy portrait, she had no difficulty in endowing him with all the good qualities I had pictured. Of course Mdlle. X. C. V. would have fallen in love if I had never written her a letter in verse, but she would have done so in a different manner, and probably with different results.

As soon as dinner was served we were summoned to do justice to the choice fish which M. de la Popeliniere had provided. Madame X. C. V. a narrowminded Greek, was naturally bigoted and superstitious. In the mind of a silly woman the idea of an alliance between the most opposite of beings, God and the Devil, seems quite natural. A priest had told her that, since she had converted her husband, her salvation was secure, for the Scriptures solemnly promised a soul for a soul to every one who would lead a heretic or a heathen within the fold of the church. And as Madame X. C. V. had converted her husband, she felt no anxiety about the life of the world to come, as she had done all that was necessary. However, she ate fish on the days appointed; the reason being that she preferred it to flesh.

Dinner over, I returned to the lady's bedside, and there stayed till nearly nine o'clock, keeping my passions well under control all the time. I was foppish enough to think that her feelings were as lively as mine, and I did not care to shew myself less self-restrained than she, though I knew then, as I know now, that this was a false line of argument. It is the same with opportunity as with fortune; one must seize them when they come to us, or else they go by, often to return no more.

Not seeing Farsetti at the table, I suspected there had been a quarrel, and I asked my sweetheart about it; but she told me I was mistaken in supposing they had quarreled with him, and that the reason of his absence was that he would never leave his house on a Friday. The deluded man had had his horoscope drawn, and learning by it that he would be assassinated on a Friday he resolved always to shut himself up on that day. He was laughed at, but persisted in the same course till he died four years ago at the age of seventy. He thought to prove by the success of his precautions that a man's destiny depends on his discretion, and on the precautions he takes to avoid the misfortunes of which he has had warning. The line of argument holds good in all cases except when the misfortunes are predicted in a horoscope; for either the ills predicted are avoidable, in which case the horoscope is a useless piece of folly, or else the horoscope is the interpreter of destiny, in which case all the precautions in the world are of no avail. The Chevalier Farsetti was therefore a fool to imagine he had proved anything at all. He would have proved a good deal for many people if he had gone out on a Friday, and had chanced to have been assassinated. Picas de la Mirandola, who believed in astrology, says, "I have no doubt truly, 'Astra influunt, non cogunt.'" But would it have been a real proof of the truth of astrology, if Farsetti had been assassinated on a Friday? In my opinion, certainly not.

The Comte d'Eigreville had introduced me to his sister, the Comtesse du Remain, who had been wanting to make my acquaintance ever since she had heard of my oracle. It was not long before I made friends with her husband and her two daughters, the elder of whom, nicknamed "Cotenfau," married M. de Polignac later on. Madame du Remain was handsome rather than pretty, but she won the love of all by her kindness, her frank courtesy, and her eagerness to be of service to her friends. She had a magnificent figure, and would have awed the whole bench of judges if she had pleaded before them.

At her house I got to know Mesdames de Valbelle and de Rancerolles, the Princess de Chimai, and many others who were then in the best society of Paris. Although Madame du Remain was not a proficient in the occult sciences, she had nevertheless consulted my oracle more frequently than Madame d'Urfe. She was of the utmost service to me in connection with an unhappy circumstance of which I shall speak presently.

The day after my long conversation with Mdlle. X. C. V., my servant told me that there was a young man waiting who wanted to give me a letter with his own hands. I had him in, and on my asking him from whom the letter came, he replied that I should find all particulars in the letter, and that he had orders to wait for an answer. The epistle ran as follows:

"I am writing this at two o'clock in the morning. I am weary and in need of rest, but a burden on my soul deprives me of sleep. The secret I am about to tell you will no longer be so grievous when I have confided in you; I shall feel eased by placing it in your breast. I am with child, and my situation drives me to despair. I was obliged to write to you because I felt I could not say it. Give me a word in reply."

My feelings on reading the above may be guessed. I was petrified with astonishment and could only write, "I will be with you at eleven o'clock."

No one should say that he has passed through great misfortunes unless they have proved too great for his mind to bear. The confidence of Mdlle. X. C. V. shewed me that she was in need of support. I congratulated myself on having the preference, and I vowed to do my best for her did it cost me my life. These were the thoughts of a lover, but for all that I could not conceal from myself the imprudence of the step she had taken. In such cases as these there is always the choice between speaking or writing, and the only feeling which can give the preference to writing is false shame, at bottom mere cowardice. If I had not been in love with her, I should have found it easier to have refused my aid in writing than if she had spoken to me, but I loved her to distraction.

"Yes," said I to myself, "she can count on me. Her mishap makes her all the dearer to me."

And below this there was another voice, a voice which whispered to me that if I succeeded in saving her my reward was sure. I am well aware that more than one grave moralist will fling stones at me for this avowal, but my answer is that such men cannot be in love as I was.

I was punctual to my appointment, and found the fair unfortunate at the door of the hotel.

"You are going out, are you? Where are you going?"

"I am going to mass at the Church of the Augustinians."

"Is this a saint's day?"

"No; but my mother makes me go every day."

"I will come with you."

"Yes do, give me your arm; we will go into the cloisters and talk there."

Mdlle. X. C. V. was accompanied by her maid, but she knew better than to be in the way, so we left her in the cloisters. As soon as we were alone she said to me,

"Have you read my letter?"

"Yes, of course; here it is, burn it yourself."

"No, keep it, and do so with your own hands."

"I see you trust in me, and I assure you I will not abuse your trust."

"I am sure you will not. I am four months with child; I can doubt it no longer, and the thought maddens me!"

"Comfort yourself, we will find some way to get over it."

"Yes; I leave all to you. You must procure an abortion."

"Never, dearest! that is a crime!"

"Alas! I know that well; but it is not a greater crime than suicide, and there lies my choice: either to destroy the wretched witness of my shame, or to poison myself. For the latter alternative I have everything ready. You are my only friend, and it is for you to decide which it shall be. Speak to me! Are you angry that I have not gone to the Chevalier Farsetti before you?"

She saw my astonishment, and stopped short, and tried to wipe away the tears which escaped from her eyes. My heart bled for her.

"Laying the question of crime on one side," said I, "abortion is out of our power. If the means employed are not violent they are uncertain, and if they are violent they are dangerous to the mother. I will never risk becoming your executioner; but reckon on me, I will not forsake you. Your honour is as dear to me as your life. Becalm, and henceforth think that the peril is mine, not yours. Make up your mind that I shall find some way of escape, and that there will be no need to cut short that life, to preserve which I would gladly die. And allow me to say that when I read your note I felt glad, I could not help it, that at such an emergency you chose me before all others to be your helper. You will find that your trust was not given in vain, for no one loves you as well as I, and no one is so fain to help you. Later you shall begin to take the remedies I will get for you, but I warn you to be on your guard, for this is a serious matter—one of life and death. Possibly you have already told somebody about it—your maid or one of your sisters?"

"I have not told anybody but you, not even the author of my shame. I tremble when I think what my mother would do and say if she found out my situation. I am afraid she will draw her conclusions from my shape."

"So far there is nothing to be observed in that direction, the beauty of the outline still remains intact."

"But every day increases its size, and for that reason we must be quick in what we do. You must find a surgeon who does not know my name and take me to him to be bled."

"I will not run the risk, it might lead to the discovery of the whole affair. I will bleed you myself; it is a simple operation."

"How grateful I am to you! I feel as if you had already brought me from death to life. What I should like you to do would be to take me to a midwife's. We can easily go without attracting any notice at the first ball at the opera."

"Yes, sweetheart, but that step is not necessary, and it might lead to our betrayal."

"No, no, in this great town there are midwives in every quarter, and we should never be known; we might keep our masks on all the time. Do me this kindness. A midwife's opinion is certainly worth having."

I could not refuse her request, but I made her agree to wait till the last ball, as the crowd was always greater, and we had a better chance of going out free from observation. I promised to be there in a black domino with a white mask in the Venetian fashion, and a rose painted beside the left eye. As soon as she saw me go out she was to follow me into a carriage. All this was carried out, but more of it anon.

I returned with her, and dined with them without taking any notice of Farsetti, who was also at the table, and had seen me come back from mass with her. We did not speak a word to one another; he did not like me and I despised him.

I must here relate a grievous mistake of which I was guilty, and which I have not yet forgiven myself.

I had promised to take Mdlle. X. C. V. to a midwife, but I certainly ought to have taken her to a respectable woman's, for all we wanted to know was how a pregnant woman should regulate her diet and manner of living. But my evil genius took me by the Rue St. Louis, and there I saw the Montigni entering her house with a pretty girl whom I did not know, and so out of curiosity I went in after them. After amusing myself there, with Mdlle. X. C. V. running in my head all the time, I asked the woman to give me the address of a midwife, as I wanted to consult one. She told me of a house in the Marais, where according to her dwelt the pearl of midwives, and began telling me some stories of her exploits, which all went to prove that the woman was an infamous character. I took her address, however, and as I should have to go there by night, I went the next day to see where the house was.

Mdlle. X. C. V. began to take the remedies which I brought her, which ought to have weakened and destroyed the result of love, but as she did not experience any benefit, she was impatient to consult a midwife. On the night of the last ball she recognized me as we had agreed, and followed me out into the coach she saw me enter, and in less than a quarter of an hour we reached the house of shame.

A woman of about fifty received us with great politeness, and asked what she could do.

Mdlle. X. C. V. told her that she believed herself pregnant, and that she desired some means of concealing her misfortune. The wretch answered with a smile that she might as well tell her plainly that it would be easy to procure abortion. "I will do your business," said she, "for fifty Louis, half to be paid in advance on account of drugs, and the rest when it's all over. I will trust in your honesty, and you will have to trust in mine. Give me the twenty-five Louis down, and come or send to-morrow for the drugs, and instructions for using them."

So saying she turned up her clothes without any ceremony, and as I, at Mdlle. X. C. V.'s request, looked away, she felt her and pronounced, as she let down her dress, that she was not beyond the fourth month.

"If my drugs," said she, "contrary to my expectation, do not do any good, we will try some other ways, and, in any case, if I do not succeed in obliging you I will return you your money."

"I don't doubt it for a moment," said I, "but would you tell me what are those other ways!"

"I should tell the lady how to destroy the foetus."

I might have told her that to kill the child meant giving a mortal wound to the mother, but I did not feel inclined to enter into a argument with this vile creature.

"If madame decides on taking your advice," said I, "I will bring you the money for drugs to-morrow."

I gave her two Louis and left. Mdlle. X. C. V. told me that she had no doubt of the infamy of this woman, as she was sure it was impossible to destroy the offspring without the risk of killing the mother also. "My only trust," said she, "is in you." I encouraged her in this idea, dissuading her from any criminal attempts, and assured her over and over again that she should not find her trust in me misplaced. All at once she complained of feeling cold, and asked if we had not time to warm ourselves in Little Poland, saying that she longed to see my pretty house. I was surprised and delighted with the idea. The night was too dark for her to see the exterior charms of my abode, she would have to satisfy herself with the inside, and leave the rest to her imagination. I thought my hour had come. I made the coach stop and we got down and walked some way, and then took another at the corner of the Rue de la Ferannerie. I promised the coachman six francs beyond his fare, and in a quarter of an hour he put us down at my door.

I rang with the touch of the master, the Pearl opened the door, and told me that there was nobody within, as I very well knew, but it was her habit to do so.

"Quick!" said I, "light us a fire, and bring some glasses and a bottle of champagne."

"Would you like an omelette?"

"Very well."

"Oh, I should like an omelette so much!" said Mdlle. X. C. V. She was ravishing, and her laughing air seemed to promise me a moment of bliss. I sat down before the blazing fire and made her sit on my knee, covering her with kisses which she gave me back as lovingly. I had almost won what I wanted when she asked me in a sweet voice to stop. I obeyed, thinking it would please her, feeling sure that she only delayed my victory to make it more complete, and that she would surrender after the champagne. I saw love, kindness, trust, and gratitude shining in her face, and I should have been sorry for her to think that I claimed her as a mere reward. No, I wanted her love, and nothing but her love.

At last we got to our last glass of champagne, we rose from the table, and sentimentally but with gentle force I laid her on a couch and held her amorously in my arms. But instead of giving herself up to my embraces she resisted them, at first by those prayers which usually make lovers more enterprising, then by serious remonstrances, and at last by force. This was too much, the mere idea of using violence has always shocked me, and I am still of opinion that the only pleasure in the amorous embrace springs from perfect union and agreement. I pleaded my cause in every way, I painted myself as the lover flattered, deceived, despised! At last I told her that I had had a cruel awakening, and I saw that the shaft went home. I fell on my knees and begged her to forgive me. "Alas!" said she, in a voice full of sadness, "I am no longer mistress of my heart, and have far greater cause for grief than you." The tears flowed fast down her cheeks, her head rested on my shoulder, and our lips met; but for all that the piece was over. The idea of renewing the attack never came into my head, and if it had I should have scornfully rejected it. After a long silence, of which we both stood in need, she to conquer her shame, and I to repress my anger, we put on our masks and returned to the opera. On our way she dared to tell me that she should be obliged to decline my friendship if she had to pay for it so dearly.

"The emotions of love," I replied, "should yield to those of honour, and your honour as well as mine require us to continue friends. What I would have done for love I will now do for devoted friendship, and for the future I will die rather than make another attempt to gain those favours of which I thought you deemed me worthy."

We separated at the opera, and the vast crowd made me lose sight of her in an instant. Next day she told me that she had danced all night. She possibly hoped to find in that exercise the cure which no medicine seemed likely to give her.

I returned to my house in a bad humour, trying in vain to justify a refusal which seemed humiliating and almost incredible. My good sense shewed me, in spite of all sophisms, that I had been grievously insulted. I recollected the witty saying of Populia, who was never unfaithful to her husband except when she was with child; "Non tollo vectorem," said she, "nisi navi plena."

I felt certain that I was not loved, and the thought grieved me; and I considered that it would be unworthy of me to love one whom I could no longer hope to possess. I resolved to avenge myself by leaving her to her fate, feeling that I could not allow myself to be duped as I had been.

The night brought wisdom with it, and when I awoke in the morning my mind was calm and I was still in love. I determined to act generously by the unfortunate girl. Without my aid she would be ruined; my course, then, would be to continue my services and to shew myself indifferent to her favours. The part was no easy one, but I played it right well, and at last my reward came of itself.

III

I Continue My Relations with Mdlle. X. C. V.—Vain
Attempts to Procure Abortion—The Aroph—She Flies
from Home and Takes Refuge in a Convent

The difficulties I encountered only served to increase my love for my charming Englishwoman. I went to see her every morning, and as my interest in her condition was genuine, she could have no suspicion that I was acting a part, or attribute my care of her to anything but the most delicate feelings. For her part she seemed well pleased in the alteration of my behaviour, though her satisfaction may very probably have been assumed. I understood women well enough to know that though she did not love me she was probably annoyed at seeing my new character sit upon me so easily.

One morning in the midst of an unimportant and disconnected conversation, she complimented me upon my strength of mind in subduing my passion, adding, with a smile, that my desire could not have pricked me very sharply, seeing that I had cured myself so well in the course of a week. I quietly replied that I owed my cure not to the weakness of my passion but to my self-respect.

"I know my own character," I said, "and without undue presumption, I think I may say that I am worthy of a woman's love. Naturally, after your convincing me that you think differently, I feel humiliated and indignant. Do you know what effect such feelings have on the heart?"

"Alas!" said she, "I know too well. Their effect is to inspire one with contempt for her who gave rise to them."

"That is going too far, at least in my case. My indignation was merely succeeded by a renewed confidence in myself, and a determination to be revenged."

"To be revenged! In what way?"

"I wish to compel you to esteem me, by proving to you that I am lord of myself, and can pass by with indifference what I once so ardently desired. I do not know whether I have succeeded yet, but I may say that I can now contemplate your charms without desiring to possess them."

"You are making a mistake, for I never ceased to esteem you, and I esteemed you as much a week ago as I do to-day. Nor for a moment I did think you capable of leaving me to my fate as a punishment for having refused to give way to your transports, and I am glad that I read your character rightly."

We went on to speak of the opiate I made her take, and as she saw no change in her condition she wanted me to increase the dose—a request I took care not to grant, as I knew that more than half a drachm might kill her. I also forbade her to bleed herself again, as she might do herself a serious injury without gaining anything by it. Her maid, of whom she had been obliged to make a confidante, had had her bled by a student, her lover. I told Mdlle. X. C. V. that if she wanted these people to keep her counsel she must be liberal with them, and she replied that she had no money. I offered her money and she accepted fifty louis, assuring me that she would repay me that sum which she needed for her brother Richard. I had not as much money about me, but I sent her the same day a packet of twelve hundred francs with a note in which I begged her to have recourse to me in all her necessities. Her brother got the money, and thought himself authorized to apply to me for aid in a much more important matter.

He was a young man and a profligate, and had got into a house of ill-fame, from which he came out in sorry plight. He complained bitterly that M. Farsetti had refused to lend him four louis, and he asked me to speak to his mother that she might pay for his cure. I consented, but when his mother heard what was the matter with him, she said it would be much better to leave him as he was, as this was the third time he had been in this condition, and that to have him cured was a waste of money, as no sooner was he well than he began his dissipated life afresh. She was quite right, for I had him cured at my expense by an able surgeon, and he was in the same way a month after. This young man seemed intended by nature for shameful excesses, for at the age of fourteen he was an accomplished profligate.

His sister was now six months with child, and as her figure grew great so did her despair. She resolved not to leave her bed, and it grieved me to see her thus cast down. Thinking me perfectly cured of my passion for her, she treated me purely as a friend, making me touch her all over to convince me that she dare not shew herself any longer. I played in short the part of a midwife, but with what a struggle! I had to pretend to be calm and unconcerned when I was consumed with passion. She spoke of killing herself in a manner that made me shudder, as I saw that she had reflected on what she was saying. I was in a difficult position when fortune came to my assistance in a strange and amusing manner.

One day, as I was dining with Madame d'Urfe, I asked her if she knew of any way by which a girl, who had allowed her lover to go too far, might be protected from shame. "I know of an infallible method," she replied, "the aroph of Paracelsus to wit, and it is easy of application. Do you wish to know more about it?" she added; and without waiting for me to answer she brought a manuscript, and put it in my hands. This powerful emmenagogue was a kind of unguent composed of several drugs, such as saffron, myrrh, etc., compounded with virgin honey. To obtain the necessary result one had to employ a cylindrical machine covered with extremely soft skin, thick enough to fill the opening of the vagina, and long enough to reach the opening of the reservoir or case containing the foetus. The end of this apparatus was to be well anointed with aroph, and as it only acted at a moment of uterine excitement it was necessary to apply it with the same movement as that of coition. The dose had to be repeated five or six times a day for a whole week.

This nostrum, and the manner of administering it, struck me in so laughable a light that I could not keep my countenance. I laughed with all my heart, but for all that I spent the next two hours in reading the dreams of Paracelsus, in which Madame d'Urfe put more trust than in the truths of the Gospel; I afterwards referred to Boerhaave, who speaks of the aroph in more reasonable terms.

Seeing, as I have remarked, the charming X. C. V. several hours a day without any kind of constraint, feeling in love with her all the time, and always restraining my feelings, it is no wonder if the hidden fire threatened at every moment to leap up from the ashes of its concealment. Her image pursued me unceasingly, of her I always thought, and every day made it more evident that I should know rest no more till I succeeded in extinguishing my passion by obtaining possession of all her charms.

As I was thinking of her by myself I resolved to tell her of my discovery, hoping she would need my help in the introduction of the cylinder. I went to see her at ten o'clock, and found her, as usual, in bed; she was weeping because the opiate I gave her did not take effect. I thought the time a good one for introducing the aroph of Paracelsus, which I assured her was an infallible means of attaining the end she desired; but whilst I was singing the praises of this application the idea came into my head to say that, to be absolutely certain, it was necessary for the aroph to be mingled with semen which had not lost its natural heat.

GIACOMO CASANOVA

"This mixture," said I, "moistening several times a day the opening of the womb, weakens it to such a degree that the foetus is expelled by its own weight."

To these details I added lengthy arguments to persuade her of the efficacy of this cure, and then, seeing that she was absorbed in thought, I said that as her lover was away she would want a sure friend to live in the same house with her, and give her the dose according to the directions of Paracelsus.

All at once she burst into a peal of laughter, and asked me if I had been jesting all the time.

I thought the game was up. The remedy was an absurd one, on the face of it; and if her common sense told her as much it would also make her guess my motive. But what limits are there to the credulity of a woman in her condition?

"If you wish," said I, persuasively, "I will give you the manuscript where all that I have said is set down plainly. I will also shew you what Boerhaeve thinks about it."

I saw that these words convinced her; they had acted on her as if by magic, and I went on while the iron was hot.

"The aroph," said I, "is the most powerful agent for bringing on menstruation."

"And that is incompatible with the state I am now in; so the aroph should procure me a secret deliverance. Do you know its composition?"

"Certainly; it is quite a simple preparation composed of certain ingredients which are well known to me, and which have to be made into a paste with butter or virgin honey. But this composition must touch the orifice of the uterus at a moment of extreme excitement."

"But in that case it seems to me that the person who gives the dose must be in love."

"Certainly, unless he is a mere animal requiring only physical incentives."

She was silent for some time, for though she was quick-witted enough, a woman's natural modesty and her own frankness, prevented her from guessing at my artifice. I, too, astonished at my success in making her believe this fable, remained silent.

At last, breaking the silence, she said, sadly,

"The method seems to me an excellent one, but I do not think I ought to make use of it."

Then she asked me if the aroph took much time to make.

"Two hours at most," I answered, "if I succeed in procuring English saffron, which Paracelsus prefers to the Oriental saffron."

At that moment her mother and the Chevalier Farsetti came in, and after some talk of no consequence she asked me to stay to dinner. I was going to decline, when Mdlle. X. C. V. said she would sit at table, on which I accepted; and we all left the room to give her time to dress. She was not long in dressing, and when she appeared her figure seemed to me quite nymph-like. I was astonished, and could scarcely believe my eyes, and I was on the point of thinking that I had been imposed on, for I could not imagine how she could manage to conceal the fulness I had felt with my own hands.

M. Farsetti sat by her, and I by the mother. Mdlle. X. C. V., whose head was full of the aroph, asked her neighbour, who gave himself out for a great chemist, if he knew it.

"I fancy I know it better than anyone," answered Farsetti, in a self-satisfied manner.

"What is it good for?"

"That is too vague a question."

"What does the word mean?"

"It is an Arabic word, of which I do not know the meaning; but no doubt Paracelsus would tell us."

"The word," said I, "is neither Arabic nor Hebrew, nor, indeed, of any language at all. It is a contraction which conceals two other words."

"Can you tell us what they are?" said the chevalier.

"Certainly; aro comes from aroma, and ph is the initial of philosophorum:"

"Did you get that out of Paracelsus?" said Farsetti, evidently annoyed.

"No, sir; I saw it in Boerhaave."

"That's good," said he, sarcastically; "Boerhaave says nothing of the sort, but I like a man who quotes readily."

"Laugh, sir, if you like," said I, proudly, "but here is the test of what I say; accept the wager if you dare. I don't quote falsely, like persons who talk of words being Arabic."

So saying I flung a purse of gold on the table, but Farsetti, who was by no means sure of what he was saying, answered disdainfully that he never betted.

However, Mdlle. X. C. V., enjoying his confusion, told him that was the best way never to lose, and began to joke him on his Arabic derivation. But, for my part, I replaced my purse in my pocket, and on some trifling pretext went out and sent my servant to Madame d'Urfe's to get me Boerhaave.

On my return to the room I sat down again at table, and joined gaily in the conversation till the return of my messenger with the book. I opened it, and as I had been reading it the evening before I soon found the place I wanted, and giving it to him begged him to satisfy himself that I had quoted not readily but exactly. Instead of taking the book, he got up and went out without saying a word.

"He has gone away in a rage," said the mother; "and I would wager anything that he will not come back again."

"I wager he will," said the daughter, "he will honour us with his agreeable company before to-morrow's sun has set."

She was right. From that day Farsetti became my determined enemy, and let no opportunity slip of convincing me of his hatred.

After dinner we all went to Passy to be present at a concert given by M. de la Popeliniere, who made us stay to supper. I found there Silvia and her charming daughter, who pouted at me and not without cause, as I had neglected her. The famous adept, St. Germain, enlivened the table with his wild tirades so finely delivered. I have never seen a more intellectual or amusing charlatan than he.

Next day I shut myself up to answer a host of questions that Esther had sent me. I took care to answer all those bearing on business matters as obscurely as possible, not only for the credit of the oracle, but also for fear of misleading the father and making him lose money. The worthy man was the most honest of Dutch millionaires, but he might easily make a large hole in his fortune, if he did not absolutely ruin himself, by putting an implicit trust in my infallibility. As for Esther, I confess that she was now no more to me than a pleasant memory.

In spite of my pretence of indifference, my whole heart was given to Mdlle. X. C. V., and I dreaded the moment when she would be no longer able to hide her condition from her family. I was sorry for having spoken about the aroph, as three days had gone by without her mentioning it, and I could not very well reopen the question myself. I was afraid that she suspected my motives, and that the esteem she professed for me had been replaced by a much less friendly sentiment. I felt that her scorn would be too much for me to bear. So humiliated was I that I could not visit her, and I doubt if I should have seen her again if she had not intervened. She wrote me a note, in which she said I was her only friend, and that the only mark of friendship she wanted was that I should come and see her every day, if it were but for a moment. I hasted to take her my reply in my own person, and promised not to neglect her, assuring her that at all hazards she might rely on me. I flattered myself that she would mention the aroph, but she did not do so. I concluded that, after thinking it over, she had resolved to think no more about it.

"Would you like me," I said, "to invite your mother and the rest of you to dine with me?"

"I shall be delighted," she replied. "It will be a forbidden pleasure to me before long."

I gave them a dinner both sumptuous and delicate. I had spared no expense to have everything of the best. I had asked Silvia, her charming daughter, an Italian musician named Magali, with whom a sister of Mdlle. X. C. V.'s was taken, and the famous bass La Garde. Mdlle. X. C. V. was in the highest spirits all the time. Sallies of wit, jests, good stories and enjoyment, were the soul of the banquet. We did not separate till midnight, and before leaving Mdlle. X. C. V. found a moment to whisper to me to come and see her early next morning, as she wanted to speak to me on matters of importance.

It will be guessed that I accepted the invitation. I waited on her before eight o'clock. She was very melancholy, and told me that she was in despair, that la Popeliniere pressed on the marriage, and that her mother persecuted her.

"She tells me that I must sign the contract, and that the dressmaker will soon be coming to take my measure for my wedding dress. To that I cannot consent, for a dressmaker would certainly see my situation. I will die rather than confide in my mother, or marry before I am delivered."

"There is always time enough to talk about dying," said I, "when all other means have failed. I think you could easily get rid of la Popeliniere, who is a man of honour. Tell him how you are situated, and he will act without compromising you, as his own interest is sufficiently involved to make him keep the secret."

"But should I be much better off then? And how about my mother?"

"Your mother? Oh! I will make her listen to reason."

"You know not what she is like. The honour of the family would oblige her to get me out of the way, but before that she would make me suffer torments to which death is preferable by far. But why have you said no more about the aroph? Is it not all a jest? It would be a very cruel one."

"On the contrary, I believe it to be infallible, though I have never been a witness of its effects; but what good is it for me to speak to you? You can guess that a delicacy of feeling has made me keep silence. Confide in your lover, who is at Venice; write him a letter, and I will take care that it is given into his hands, in five or six days, by a sure messenger. If he is not well off I will give you whatever money may be needed for him to come without delay, and save your honour and life by giving you the aroph."

"This idea is a good one and the offer generous on your part, but it is not feasible, as you would see if you knew more about my circumstances. Do not think any more of my lover; but supposing I made up my mind to receive the aroph from another, tell me how it could be done. Even if my lover were in Paris, how could he spend an entire week with me, as he would have to? And how could he give me the dose five or six times a day for a week? You see yourself that this remedy is out of the question."

"So you would give yourself to another, if you thought that would save your honour?"

"Certainly, if I were sure that the thing would be kept secret. But where shall I find such a person? Do you think he would be easy to find, or that I can go and look for him?"

I did not know what to make of this speech; for she knew I loved her, and I did not see why she should put herself to the trouble of going far when what she wanted was to her hand. I was inclined to think that she wanted me to ask her to make choice of myself as the administrator of the remedy, either to spare her modesty, or to have the merit of yielding to my love and thus obliging me to be grateful; but I might be wrong, and I did not care to expose myself to the humiliation of a refusal. On the other hand I could hardly think she wanted to insult me. Not knowing what to say or which way to turn, and wanting to draw an explanation from her, I sighed profoundly, took up my hat, and made as if I were going, exclaiming, "Cruel girl, my lot is more wretched than yours."

She raised herself in the bed and begged me with tears in her eyes to remain, and asked me how I could call myself more wretched than her. Pretending to be annoyed and yet full of love for her, I told her that the contempt in which she held me had affected me deeply, since in her necessity she preferred the offices of one who was unknown to her rather than make use of me.

"You are cruel and unjust," she said, weeping. "I see, for my part, that you love me no longer since you wish to take advantage of my cruel necessity to gain a triumph over me. This is an act of revenge not worthy of a man of feeling."

Her tears softened me, and I fell on my knees before her.

"Since you know, dearest, that I worship you, how can you think me capable of revenging myself on you? Do you think that I can bear to hear you say that since your lover cannot help you you do not know where to look for help?"

"But after refusing you my favours, could I ask this office of you with any decency? Have I not good reason to be afraid that as I refused to take pity on your love so you would refuse to take pity on my necessity?"

"Do you think that a passionate lover ceases to love on account of a refusal which may be dictated by virtue? Let me tell you all I think. I confess I once thought you did not love me, but now I am sure of the contrary; and that your heart would have led you to satisfy my love, even if you had not been thus situated. I may add that you no doubt feel vexed at my having any doubts of your love."

"You have interpreted my feelings admirably. But how we are to be together with the necessary freedom from observation remains to be seen."

"Do not be afraid. Now I am sure of your consent, it will not be long before I contrive some plan. In the meanwhile I will go and make the aroph."

I had resolved that if ever I succeeded in persuading Mdlle. X. C. V. to make use of my specific I would use nothing but honey, so the composition of the aroph would not be a very complicated process. But if one point was then plain and simple, another remained to be solved, and its solution gave me some difficulty. I should have to pass several nights in continual toils. I feared I had promised more than I could perform, and I should not be able to make any abatement without hazarding, not the success of the aroph, but the bliss I had taken such pains to win. Again, as her younger sister slept in the same room with her and close to her, the operation could not be performed there. At last chance—a divinity which often helps lovers—came to my aid.

I was obliged to climb up to the fourth floor and met the scullion on my way, who guessed where I was going, and begged me not to go any farther as the place was taken.

"But," said I, "you have just come out of it."

"Yes, but I only went in and came out again."

"Then I will wait till the coast is clear."

"For goodness' sake, sir, do not wait!"

"Ah, you rascal! I see what is going on. Well I will say nothing about it, but I must see her."

"She won't come out, for she heard your steps and shut herself in."

"She knows me, does she?"

"Yes, and you know her."

"All right, get along with you! I won't say anything about it."

He went down, and the idea immediately struck me that the adventure might be useful to me. I went up to the top, and through a chink I saw Madelaine, Mdlle. X. C. V.'s maid. I reassured her, and promised to keep the secret, whereon she opened the door, and after I had given her a louis, fled in some confusion. Soon after, I came down, and the scullion who was waiting for me on the landing begged me to make Madelaine give him half the louis.

"I will give you one all to yourself," said I, "if you will tell me the story"—an offer which pleased the rogue well enough. He told me the tale of his loves, and said he always spent the night with her in the garret, but that for three days they had been deprived of their pleasures, as madam had locked the door and taken away the key. I made him shew me the place, and looking through the keyhole I saw that there was plenty of room for a mattress. I gave the scullion a Louis, and went away to ripen my plans.

It seemed to me that there was no reason why the mistress should not sleep in the garret as well as the maid. I got a picklock and several skeleton keys, I put in a tin box several doses of the aroph-that is, some honey mixed with pounded stag's horn to make it thick enough, and the next morning I went to the "Hotel de Bretagne," and immediately tried my picklock. I could have done without it, as the first skeleton key I tried opened the wornout lock.

Proud of my idea, I went down to see Mdlle. X. C. V., and in a few words told her the plan.

"But," said she, "I should have to go through Madelaine's room to get to the garret."

"In that case, dearest, we must win the girl over."

"Tell her my secret?"

"Just so."

"Oh, I couldn't!"

"I will see to it; the golden key opens all doors."

The girl consented to all I asked her, but the scullion troubled me, for if he found us out he might be dangerous. I thought, however, that I might trust to Madelaine, who was a girl of wit, to look after him.

Before going I told the girl that I wanted to discuss some important matters with her, and I told her to meet me in the cloisters of the Augustinian Church. She came at the appointed time and I explained to her the whole plan in all its details. She soon understood me, and after telling me that she would take care to put her own bed in the new kind of boudoir, she added that, to be quite safe, we must make sure of the scullion.

"He is a sharp lad," said Madelaine, "and I think I can answer for him. However, you may leave that to me."

I gave her the key and six louis, bidding her inform her mistress of what we had agreed upon, and get the garret ready to receive us. She went away quite merry. A maid who is in love is never so happy as when she can make her mistress protect her intrigues.

Next morning the scullion called on me at my house. The first thing I told him was to take care not to betray himself to my servants, and never to come and see me except in a case of necessity. He promised discretion, and assured me of his devotion to my service. He gave me the key of the garret and told me that he had got another. I admired his forethought, and gave him a present of six louis, which had more effect on him than the finest words.

Next morning I only saw Mdlle. X. C. V. for a moment to warn her that I should be at the appointed place at ten that evening. I went there early without being seen by anybody. I was in a cloak, and carried in my pocket the aroph, flint and steel, and a candle. I found a good bed, pillows, and a thick coverlet—a very useful provision, as the nights were cold, and we should require some sleep in the intervals of the operation.

At eleven a slight noise made my heart begin to beat—always a good sign. I went out, and found my mistress by feeling for her, and reassured her by a tender kiss. I brought her in, barricaded the door, and took care to cover up the keyhole to baffle the curious, and, if the worse happened, to avoid a surprise.

On my lighting the candle she seemed uneasy, and said that the light might discover us if anybody came up to the fourth floor.

"That's not likely," I said; "and besides, we can't do without it, for how am I to give you the aroph in the dark?"

"Very good," she replied, "we can put it out afterwards."

Without staying for those preliminary dallyings which are so sweet when one is at ease, we undressed ourselves, and began with all seriousness to play our part, which we did to perfection. We looked like a medical student about to perform an operation, and she like a patient, with this difference that it was the patient who arranged the dressing. When she was ready—that is, when she had placed the aroph as neatly as a skull-cap fits a parson—she put herself in the proper position for the preparation to mix with the semen.

The most laughable part of it all was that we were both as serious as two doctors of divinity.

When the introduction of the aroph was perfect the timid lady put out the candle, but a few minutes after it had to be lighted again. I told her politely that I was delighted to begin again, and the voice in which I paid her this compliment made us both burst into laughter.

I didn't take so short a time over my second operation as my first, and my sweetheart, who had been a little put out, was now quite at her ease.

Her modesty had now been replaced by confidence, and as she was looking at the aroph fitted in its place, she shewed me with her pretty finger very evident signs of her co-operation in the work. Then with an affectionate air, she asked me if I would not like to rest, as we had still a good deal to do before our work was at an end.

"You see," said I, "that I do not need rest, and I think we had better set to again."

No doubt she found my reason a good one, for, without saying anything, she put herself ready to begin again, and afterwards we took a good long sleep. When I woke up, feeling as fresh as ever, I asked her to try another operation; and after carrying this through successfully, I determined to be guided by her and take care of myself, for we had to reserve our energies for the following nights. So, about four o'clock in the morning she left me, and softly made her way to her room, and at daybreak I left the hotel under the protection of the scullion, who took me by a private door I did not know of.

About noon, after taking an aromatic bath, I went to call on Mdlle. X. C. V., whom I found sitting up in bed as usual, elegantly attired, and with a happy smile on her lips. She spoke at such length on her gratitude, and thanked me so often, that, believing myself, and with good cause, to be her debtor, I began to get impatient.

"Is it possible," I said, "that you do not see how degrading your thanks are to me? They prove that you do not love me, or that if you love me, you think my love less strong than yours."

Our conversation then took a tender turn, and we were about to seal our mutual ardours without troubling about the aroph, when prudence bade us beware. It would not have been safe, and we had plenty of time before us. We contented ourselves with a tender embrace till the night should come.

My situation was a peculiar one, for though I was in love with this charming girl I did not feel in the least ashamed of having deceived her, especially as what I did could have no effect, the place being taken. It was my self-esteem which made me congratulate myself on the sharp practice which had procured me such pleasures. She told me that she was sorry she had denied me when I had asked her before, and said that she felt now that I had good reason to suspect the reality of her love. I did my best to reassure her, and indeed all suspicions on my part would have been but idle thoughts, as I had succeeded beyond all expectation. However, there is one point upon which I congratulate myself to this day—namely, that during those nightly toils of mine, which did so little towards the object of her desires, I succeeded in inspiring her with such a feeling of resignation that she promised, of her own accord, not to despair any more, but to trust in and be guided by me. She often told me during our nocturnal conversations that she was happy and would continue to be so, even though the aroph had no effect. Not that she had ceased to believe in it, for she continued the application of the harmless preparation till our last assaults, in which we wanted in those sweet combats to exhaust all the gifts of pleasure.

"Sweetheart," said she, just before we parted finally, "it seems to me that what we have been about is much more likely to create than to destroy, and if the aperture had not been hermetically closed we should doubtless have given the little prisoner a companion."

A doctor of the Sorbonne could not have reasoned better.

Three or four days afterwards I found her thoughtful but quiet. She told me that she had lost all hope of getting rid of her burden before the proper time. All the while, however, her mother persecuted her, and she would have to choose in a few days between making a declaration as to her state and signing the marriage contract. She would accept neither of these alternatives, and had decided on escaping from her home, and asked me to help her in doing so.

I had determined to help her, but I desired to save my reputation, for it might have been troublesome if it had been absolutely known that I had carried her off or furnished her with the means to escape. And as for any other alternative, neither of us had any idea of matrimony.

I left her and went to the Tuileries, where a sacred concert was being given. The piece was a motet composed by Moudonville, the words by the Abbe de Voisenon, whom I had furnished with the idea, "The Israelites on Mount Horeb."

As I was getting out of my carriage, I saw Madame du Remain descending alone from hers. I ran up to her, and received a hearty welcome. "I am delighted," said she, "to find you here, it is quite a piece of luck. I am going to hear this novel composition, and have two reserved seats. Will you do me the honour of accepting one?"

Although I had my ticket in my pocket I could not refuse so honourable an offer, so, giving her my arm, we walked up to two of the best places in the house.

At Paris no talking is allowed during the performance of sacred music, especially when the piece is heard for the first time; so Madame du Remain could draw no conclusions from my silence throughout the performance, but she guessed that something was the matter from the troubled and absent expression of my face, which was by no means natural to me.

"M. Casanova," said she, "be good enough to give me your company for an hour. I want to ask you-two or three questions which can only be solved by your cabala. I hope you will oblige me, as I am, very anxious to know the answers, but we must be quick as I have an engagement to sup in Paris."

It may be imagined that I did not wait to be asked twice, and as soon as we got to her house I went to work on the questions, and solved them all in less than half an hour.

When I had finished, "M. Casanova," said she, in the kindest manner possible, "what is the matter with you? You are not in your usual state of equanimity, and if I am not mistaken you are dreading some dire event. Or perhaps you are on the eve of taking some important resolution? I am not inquisitive, but if I can be of any service to you at Court, make use of me, and be sure that I will do my best. If necessary, I will go to Versailles to-morrow morning. I know all the ministers. Confide in me your troubles, if I cannot lighten them I can at least share them, and be sure I will keep your counsel."

Her words seemed to me a voice from heaven, a warning from my good genius to open my heart to this lady, who had almost read my thoughts, and had so plainly expressed her interest in my welfare.

After gazing at her for some seconds without speaking, but with a manner that shewed her how grateful I was, "Yes madam," I said, "I am indeed critically situated, may be on the serge of ruin, but your kindness has calmed my soul and made me once more acquainted with hope. You shall hear how I am placed. I am going to trust you with a secret of the most delicate description, but I can rely on your being as discreet as you are good. And if after hearing my story you deign to give me your advice, I promise to follow it and never to divulge its author."

After this beginning, which gained her close attention, I told her all the circumstances of the case, neither concealing the young lady's name nor any of the circumstances which made it my duty to watch over her welfare. All the same I said nothing about the aroph or the share I had taken in its exhibition. The incident appeared to me too farcical for a serious drama, but I confessed that I had procured the girl drugs in the hope of relieving her of her burden.

After this weighty communication I stopped, and Madame du Rumain remained silent, as if lost in thought, for nearly a quarter of an hour. At last she rose, saying,

"I am expected at Madame de la Marque's, and I must go, as I am to meet the Bishop of Montrouge, to whom I want to speak, but I hope I shall eventually be able to help you. Come here the day after tomorrow, you will find me alone; above all, do nothing before you see me. Farewell."

I left her full of hope, and resolved to follow her advice and hers only in the troublesome affair in which I was involved.

The Bishop of Montrouge whom she was going to address on an important matter, the nature of which was well known to me, was the Abbe de Voisenon, who was thus named because he often went there. Montrouge is an estate near Paris, belonging to the Duc de la Valiere.

I saw Mdlle. X. C. V. the following day, and contented myself with telling her that in a couple of days I hope to give her some good news. I was pleased with her manner, which was full of resignation and trust in my endeavours.

The day after, I went to Madame du Rumain's punctually at eight. The porter told me that I should find the doctor with my lady, but I went upstairs all the same, and as soon as the doctor saw me he took his leave. His name was Herrenschwand, and all the ladies in Paris ran after him. Poor Poinsinet put him in a little one-act play called Le Cercle, which, though of very ordinary merit, was a great success.

"My dear sir," said Madame du Rumain, as soon as we were alone, "I have succeeded in my endeavours on your behalf, and it is now for you to keep secret my share in the matter. After I had pondered over the case of conscience you submitted to me, I went to the convent of C——where the abbess is a friend of mine, and I entrusted her with the secret, relying on her discretion. We agreed that she should receive the young lady in her convent, and give her a good lay-sister to nurse her through her confinement. Now you will not deny," said she, with a smile, "that the cloisters are of some use. Your young friend must go by herself to the convent with a letter for the abbess, which I will give her, and which she must deliver to the porter. She will then be admitted and lodged in a suitable chamber. She will receive no visitors nor any letters that have not passed through my hands. The abbess will bring her answers to me, and I will pass them on to you. You must see that her only correspondent must be yourself, and you must receive news of her welfare only through me. On your hand in writing to her you must leave the address to be filled in by me. I had to tell the abbess the lady's name, but not yours as she did not require it.

"Tell your young friend all about our plans, and when she is ready come and tell me, and I will give you the letter to the abbess. Tell her to bring nothing but what is strictly necessary, above all no diamonds or trinkets of any value. You may assure her that the abbess will be friendly, will come and see her every now and then, will give her proper books—in a word, that she will be well looked after. Warn her not to confide in the laysister who will attend on her. I have no doubt she is an excellent woman, but she is a nun, and the secret might leak out. After she is safely delivered, she must go to confession and perform her Easter duties, and the abbess will give her a certificate of good behaviour; and she can then return to her mother, who will be too happy to see her to say anything more about the marriage, which, of course, she ought to give as her reason of her leaving home."

After many expressions of my gratitude to her, and of my admiration of her plan, I begged her to give me the letter on the spot, as there was no time to be lost. She was good enough to go at once to her desk, where she wrote as follows:

"My dear abbess—The young lady who will give you this letter is the same of whom we have spoken. She wishes to spend three of four months under your protection, to recover her peace of mind, to perform her devotions, and to make sure that when she returns to her mother nothing more will be said about the marriage, which is partly the cause of her temporary separation from her family."

After reading it to me, she put it into my hands unsealed that Mdlle. X. C. V. might be able to read it. The abbess in question was a princess, and her convent was consequently a place above all suspicion. As Madame du Rumain gave me the letter, I felt such an impulse of gratitude that I fell on my knees before her. This generous woman was useful to me on another occasion, of which I shall speak later on.

After leaving Madame du Rumain I went straight to the "Hotel de Bretagne," where I saw Mdlle. X. C. V., who had only time to tell me that she was engaged for the rest of the day, but that she would come to the garret at eleven o'clock that night, and that then we could talk matters over. I was overjoyed at this arrangement, as I foresaw that after this would come the awakening from a happy dream, and that I should be alone with her no more.

Before leaving the hotel I gave the word to Madelaine, who in turn got the scullion to have everything in readiness.

I kept the appointment, and had not long to wait for my mistress. After making her read the letter written by Madame du Rumain (whose name I withheld from her without her taking offence thereat) I put out the candle, and without troubling about the aroph, we set ourselves to the pleasant task of proving that we truly loved each other.

In the morning, before we separated, I gave her all the instructions I had received from Madame du Rumain; and we agreed that she should leave the house at eight o'clock with such things as she absolutely required, that she should take a coach to the Place Maubert, then send it away, and take another to the Place Antoine, and again, farther on, a third coach, in which she was to go to the convent named. I begged her not to forget to burn all the letters she had received from me, and to write to me from the convent as often as she could, to seal her letters but to leave the address blank. She promised to carry out my instructions, and I then made her accept a packet of two hundred louis, of which she might chance to be in need. She wept, more for my situation than her own, but I consoled her by saying that I had plenty of money and powerful patrons.

"I will set out," said she, "the day after to-morrow, at the hour agreed on." And thereupon, I having promised to come to the house the day after her departure, as if I knew nothing about it, and to let her know what passed, we embraced each other tenderly, and I left her.

I was troubled in thinking about her fate. She had wit and courage, but when experience is wanting wit often leads men to commit acts of great folly.

The day after the morrow I took a coach, and posted myself in a corner of the street by which she had to pass. I saw her come, get out of the coach, pay the coachman, go down a narrow street, and a few minutes after reappear again, veiled and hooded, carrying a small parcel in her hand. She then took another conveyance which went off in the direction we had agreed upon.

The day following being Low Sunday, I felt that I must present myself at the "Hotel de Bretagne," for as I went there every day before the daughter's flight I could not stop going there without strengthening any suspicions which might be entertained about me. But it was a painful task. I had to appear at my ease and cheerful in a place where I was quite sure all would be sadness and confusion. I must say that it was an affair requiring higher powers of impudence than fall to the lot of most men.

I chose a time when all the family would be together at table, and I walked straight into the dining-room. I entered with my usual cheerful manner, and sat down by madame, a little behind her, pretending not to see her surprise, which, however, was plainly to be seen, her whole face being flushed with rage and astonishment. I had not been long in the room before I asked where her daughter was. She turned round, looked me through and through, and said not a word.

"Is she ill?" said I.

"I know nothing about her."

This remark, which was pronounced in a dry manner, put me at my ease, as I now felt at liberty to look concerned. I sat there for a quarter of an hour, playing the part of grave and astonished silence, and then, rising, I asked if I could do anything, for which all my reward was a cold expression of thanks. I then left the room and went to Mdlle. X. C. V.'s chamber as if I had thought she was there, but found only Madelaine. I asked her with a meaning look where her mistress was. She replied by begging me to tell her, if I knew.

"Has she gone by herself?"

"I know nothing at all about it, sir, but they say you know all. I beg of you to leave me."

Pretending to be in the greatest astonishment, I slowly walked away and took a coach, glad to have accomplished this painful duty. After the reception I had met with I could without affectation pose as offended, and visit the family no more, for whether I were guilty or innocent, Madame X. C. V. must see that her manner had been plain enough for me to know what it meant.

I was looking out of my window at an early hour two or three days afterwards, when a coach stopped before my door, and Madame X C V-, escorted by M. Farsetti got out. I made haste to meet them on the stair, and welcomed them, saying I was glad they had done me the honour to come and take breakfast with me, pretending not to know of any other reason. I asked them to sit down before the fire, and enquired after the lady's health; but without noticing my question she said that she had not come to take breakfast, but to have some serious conversation.

"Madam," said I, "I am your humble servant; but first of all pray be seated."

She sat down, while Farsetti continued standing. I did not press him, but turning towards the lady begged her to command me.

"I am come here," she said, "to ask you to give me my daughter if she be in your power, or to tell me where she is."

"Your daughter, madam? I know nothing about her! Do you think me capable of a crime?"

"I do not accuse you of abducting her; I have not come here to reproach you nor to utter threats, I have only come to ask you to shew yourself my friend. Help me to get my daughter again this very day; you will give me my life. I am certain that you know all. You were her only confidant and her only friend; you passed hours with her every day; she must have told you of her secret. Pity a bereaved mother! So far no one knows of the facts; give her back to me and all shall be forgotten, and her honour saved."

"Madam, I feel for you acutely, but I repeat that I know nothing of your daughter."

The poor woman, whose grief touched me, fell at my feet and burst into tears. I was going to lift her from the ground, when Farsetti told her, in a voice full of indignation, that she should blush to humble herself in such a manner before a man of my description. I drew myself up, and looking at him scornfully said,

"You insolent scoundrel! What do you mean by talking of me like that?"

"Everybody is certain that you know all about it."

"Then they are impudent fools, like you. Get out of my house this instant and wait for me, I will be with you in a quarter of an hour."

So saying, I took the poor chevalier by the shoulders, and giving him sundry shakes I turned him out of the room. He came back and called to the lady to come, too, but she rose and tried to quiet me.

"You ought to be more considerate towards a lover," said she, "for he would marry my daughter now, even after what she has done."

"I am aware of the fact, madam, and I have no doubt that his courtship was one of the chief reasons which made your daughter resolve to leave her home, for she hated him even more than she hated the fermier-general."

"She has behaved very badly, but I promise not to say anything more about marrying her. But I am sure you know all about it, as you gave her fifty louis, without which she could not have done anything."

"Nay, not so."

"Do not deny it, sir; here is the evidence—a small piece of your letter to her."

She gave me a scrap of the letter I had sent the daughter, with the fifty louis for her brother. It contained the following lines,

"I hope that these wretched louis will convince you that I am ready to sacrifice everything, my life if need be, to assure you of my affection."

"I am far from disavowing this evidence of my esteem for your daughter, but to justify myself I am obliged to tell you a fact which I should have otherwise kept secret—namely, that I furnished your daughter with this sum to enable her to pay your son's debts, for which he thanked me in a letter which I can shew you."

"My son?"

"Your son, madam."

"I will make you an ample atonement for my suspicions."

Before I had time to make any objection, she ran down to fetch Farsetti, who was waiting in the courtyard, and made him come up and hear what I had just told her.

"That's not a likely tale," said the insolent fellow.

I looked at him contemptuously, and told him he was not worth convincing, but that I would beg the lady to ask her son and see whether I told the truth.

"I assure you," I added, "that I always urged your daughter to marry M. de la Popeliniere."

"How can you have the face to say that," said Farsetti, "when you talk in the letter of your affection?"

"I do not deny it," said I. "I loved her, and I was proud of my affection for her. This affection, of whatever sort it may have been (and that is not this gentleman's business), was the ordinary topic of conversation between us. If she had told me that she was going to leave her home, I should either have dissuaded her or gone with her, for I loved her as I do at this moment; but I would never have given her money to go alone."

"My dear Casanova," said the mother, "if you will help me to find her I shall believe in your innocence."

"I shall be delighted to aid you, and I promise to commence the quest to-day."

"As soon as you have any news, come and tell me."

"You may trust me to do so," said I, and we parted.

I had to play my part carefully; especially it was essential that I should behave in public in a manner consistent with my professions. Accordingly, the next day I went to M. Chaban, first commissary of police, requesting him to institute enquiries respecting the flight of Mdlle. X. C. V. I was sure that in this way the real part I had taken in the matter would be the better concealed; but the commissary, who had the true spirit of his profession, and had liked me when he first saw me six years before, began to laugh when he heard what I wanted him to do.

"Do you really want the police to discover," said he, "where the pretty Englishwoman is to be found?"

"Certainly."

It then struck me that he was trying to make me talk and to catch me tripping, and I had no doubt of it when I met Farsetti going in as I was coming out.

Next day I went to acquaint Madame X. C. V. with the steps I had taken, though as yet my efforts had not been crowned with success.

"I have been more fortunate than you," said she, "and if you will come with me to the place where my daughter has gone, and will join me in persuading her to return, all will be well."

"Certainly," said I, "I shall be most happy to accompany you."

Taking me at my word, she put on her cloak, and leaning on my arm walked along till we came to a coach. She then gave me a slip of paper, begging me to tell the coachman to drive us to the address thereon.

I was on thorns, and my heart beat fast, for I thought I should have to read out the address of the convent. I do not know what I should have done if my fears had been well grounded, but I should certainly not have gone to the convent. At last I read what was written; it was "Place Maubert," and I grew calm once more.

I told the coachman to drive us to the Place Maubert. We set off, and in a short time stopped at the opening of an obscure back street before a dirty-looking house, which did not give one a high idea of the character of its occupants. I gave Madame X. C. V. my arm, and she had the satisfaction of looking into every room in the five floors of the house, but what she sought for was not there, and I expected to see her overwhelmed with grief. I was mistaken, however. She looked distressed but satisfied, and her eyes seemed to ask pardon of me. She had found out from the coachman, who had taken her daughter on the first stage of her journey, that she had alighted in front of the house in question, and had gone down the back street. She told me that the scullion had confessed that he had taken me letters twice from his young mistress, and that Madelaine said all the time that she was sure her mistress and I were in love with each other. They played their parts well.

As soon as I had seen Madame X. C. V. safely home, I went to Madame du Rumain to tell her what had happened; and I then wrote to my fair recluse, telling her what had gone on in the world since her disappearance.

Three or four days after this date, Madame du Rumain gave me the first letter I received from Mdlle. X. C. V. She spoke in it of the quiet life she was leading, and her gratitude to me, praised the abbess and the lay-sister, and gave me the titles of the books they lent her, which she liked reading. She also informed me what money she had spent, and said she was happy in everything, almost in being forbidden to leave her room.

I was delighted with her letter, but much more with the abbess's epistle to Madame du Rumain. She was evidently fond of the girl, and could not say too much in her praise, saying how sweet-tempered, clever, and lady-like she was; winding up by assuring her friend that she went to see her every day.

I was charmed to see the pleasure this letter afforded Madame du Rumain—pleasure which was increased by the perusal of the letter I had received. The only persons who were displeased were the poor mother, the frightful Farsetti, and the old fermier, whose misfortune was talked about in the clubs, the Palais-Royal, and the coffee-houses. Everybody put me down for some share in the business, but I laughed at their gossip, believing that I was quite safe.

All the same, la Popeliniere took the adventure philosophically and made a one-act play out of it, which he had acted at his little theatre in Paris. Three months afterwards he got married to a very pretty girl, the daughter of a Bordeaux alderman. He died in the course of two years, leaving his widow pregnant with a son, who came into the world six months after the father's death. The unworthy heir to the rich man had the face to accuse the widow of adultery, and got the child declared illegitimate to the eternal shame of the court which gave this iniquitous judgment and to the grief of every honest Frenchman. The iniquitous nature of the judgment was afterwards more clearly demonstrated—putting aside the fact that nothing could be said against the mother's character—by the same court having the face to declare a child born eleven months after the father's death legitimate.

I continued for ten days to call upon Madame X. C. V., but finding myself coldly welcomed, decided to go there no more.

IV

Fresh Adventures—J. J. Rousseau—I set up a
Business—Castel—Bajac—A Lawsuit is Commenced
Against Me—M. de Sartine

Mdlle. X. C. V. had now been in the convent for a month, and her
affair had ceased to be a common topic of conversation. I thought
I should hear no more of it, but I was mistaken. I continued, however,
to amuse myself, and my pleasure in spending freely quite prevented me
from thinking about the future. The Abbe de Bernis, whom I went to
see regularly once a week, told me one day that the comptroller-general
often enquired how I was getting on. "You are wrong," said the abbe,
"to neglect him." He advised me to say no more about my claims, but
to communicate to him the means I had spoken of for increasing the
revenues of the state. I laid too great store by the advice of the man who
had made my fortune not to follow it. I went to the comptroller, and
trusting in his probity I explained my scheme to him. This was to pass
a law by which every estate, except that left by father to son, should
furnish the treasury with one year's income; every deed of gift formally
drawn up being subject to the same provision. It seemed to me that the
law could not give offence to anyone; the heir had only to imagine that
he had inherited a year later than was actually the case. The minister
was of the same opinion as myself, told me that there would not be the
slightest difficulty involved, and assured me that my fortune was made.
In a week afterwards his place was taken by M. de Silhouette, and when
I called on the new minister he told me coldly that when my scheme
became law he would tell me. It became law two years afterwards, and
when, as the originator of the scheme, I attempted to get my just reward,
they laughed in my face.

Shortly after, the Pope died, and he was succeeded by the Venetian
Rezzonico, who created my patron, the Abby de Bernis, a cardinal.
However, he had to go into exile by order of the king two days after his
gracious majesty had presented him with the red cap: so good a thing it
is to be the friend of kings!

The disgrace of my delightful abbe left me without a patron, but I
had plenty of money, and so was enabled to bear this misfortune with
resignation.

For having undone all the work of Cardinal Richelieu, for having changed the old enmity between France and Austria into friendship, for delivering Italy from the horrors of war which befell her whenever these countries had a bone to pick, although he was the first cardinal made by a pope who had had plenty of opportunities for discovering his character, merely because, on being asked, he had given it as his opinion that the Prince de Soubise was not a fit person to command the French armies, this great ecclesiastic was driven into exile. The moment the Pompadour heard of this opinion of his, she decreed his banishment—a sentence which was unpopular with all classes of society; but they consoled themselves with epigrams, and the new cardinal was soon forgotten. Such is the character of the French people; it cares neither for its own misfortunes nor for those of others, if only it can extract laughter from them.

In my time epigrammatists and poetasters who assailed ministers or even the king's mistresses were sent to the Bastille, but the wits still persisted in being amusing, and there were some who considered a jest incomplete that was not followed by a prosecution. A man whose name I have forgotten—a great lover of notoriety—appropriated the following verses by the younger Crebellon and went to the Bastille rather than disown them.

> *"All the world's upside down!*
> *Jupiter has donned the gown—the King.*
> *Venus mounts the council stair—the Pompadour.*
> *Plutus trifles with the fair—M. de Boulogne.*
> *Mercury in mail is drest—Marechal de Richelieu.*
> *Mighty Mars has turned a priest—the Duc de Clermont, abbe of*
> *St. Germain-des-pres."*

Crebillon, who was not the sort of man to conceal his writings, told the Duc de Choiseul that he had written some verses exactly like these, but that it was possible the prisoner had been inspired with precisely the same ideas. This jest was applauded, and the author of "The Sofa" was let alone.

Cardinal de Bernis passed ten years in exile, 'procul negotiis', but he was not happy, as he told me himself when I knew him in Rome fifteen years afterwards. It is said that it is better to be a minister than a king—an opinion which seems ridiculous when it is analyzed. The question is, which is the better, independence or its contrary. The axiom may possibly be verified in a despotic government under an absurd, weak, or careless king who serves as a mere mask for his master the minister; but in all other cases it is an absurdity.

Cardinal de Bernis was never recalled; there is no instance of Louis XV having ever recalled a minister whom he had disgraced; but on the death of Rezzonico he had to go to Rome to be present at the conclave, and there he remained as French ambassador.

About this time Madame d'Urfe conceived a wish to make the acquaintance of J. J. Rousseau, and we went to call upon him at Montmorenci, on the pretext of giving him music to copy—an occupation in which he was very skilled. He was paid twice the sum given to any other copyist, but he guaranteed that the work should be faultlessly done. At that period of his life copying music was the great writer's sole means of subsistence.

We found him to be a man of a simple and modest demeanour, who talked well, but who was not otherwise distinguished either intellectually or physically. We did not think him what would be called a good-natured man, and as he was far from having the manners of good society Madame d'Urfe did not hesitate to pronounce him vulgar. We saw the woman with whom he lived, and of whom we had heard, but she scarcely looked at us. On our way home we amused ourselves by talking about Rousseau's eccentric habits.

I will here note down the visit of the Prince of Conti (father of the gentleman who is now known as the Comte de la March) to Rousseau.

The prince—a good-natured man-went by himself to Montmorenci, on purpose to spend a day in conversation with the philosopher, who was even then famous. He found him in the park, accosted him, and said that he had come to dine with him and to talk without restraint.

"Your highness will fare but badly," said Rousseau: "however, I will tell them to lay another knife and fork."

The philosopher gave his instructions, and came out and rejoined the prince, with whom he walked up and down for two or three hours. When it was dinner-time he took the prince into his dining-room, where the table was laid for three.

"Who is going to dine with us?" said the prince. "I thought we were to be alone."

"The third party," said Rousseau, "is my other self—a being who is neither my wife, nor my mistress, nor my servant-maid, nor my mother, nor my daughter, but yet personates all these characters at once."

"I daresay, my dear fellow, I daresay; but as I came to dine with you alone, I will not dine with your—other self, but will leave you with all the rest of you to keep your company."

So saying the prince bade him farewell and went out. Rousseau did not try to keep him.

About this time I witnessed the failure of a play called 'Aristides' Daughter', written by the ingenious Madame de Graffini, who died of vexation five days after her play was damned. The Abbe de Voisenon was horrified, as he had advised the lady to produce it, and was thought to have had some hand in its composition, as well as in that of the 'Lettres Peruviennes' and 'Cenie'. By a curious coincidence, just about the same date, Rezzonico's mother died of joy because her son had become pope. Grief and joy kill many more women than men, which proves that if women have mere feeling than men they have also less strength.

When Madame d'Urfe thought that my adopted son was comfortably settled in Viar's house, she made me go with her and pay him a visit. I found him lodged like a prince, well dressed, made much of, and almost looked up to. I was astonished, for this was more than I had bargained for. Madame d'Urfe had given him masters of all sorts, and a pretty little pony for him to learn riding on. He was styled M. le Comte d'Aranda. A girl of sixteen, Viar's daughter, a fine-looking young woman, was appointed to look after him, and she was quite proud to call herself my lord's governess. She assured Madame d'Urfe that she took special care of him; that as soon as he woke she brought him his breakfast in bed; that she then dressed him, and did not leave his side the whole day. Madame d'Urfe approved of everything, told the girl to take even greater care of the count, and promised that she should not go unrewarded. As for the young gentleman, he was evidently quite happy, as he told me himself again and again, but I suspected a mystery somewhere, and determined that I would go and see him by myself another time and solve it.

On our journey home I told Madame d'Urfe how grateful I was for all her goodness to the boy, and that I approved of all the arrangements that had been made with the exception of the name Aranda, "which," said I, "may some day prove a thorn in his side." She answered that the lad had said enough to convince her that he had a right to bear that name. "I had," she said, "in my desk a seal with the arms of the house of Aranda, and happening to take it up I shewed it him as we shew trinkets to children to amuse them, but as soon as he saw it he burst out,

"'How came you to have my arms?'

"Your arms!" I answered. "I got this seal from the Comte d'Aranda; how can you prove that you are a scion of that race?"

"'Do not ask me, madam; my birth is a secret I can reveal to no one.'"

The imposition and above all the impudence of the young knave astounded me. I should not have thought him capable of it, and a week after I went to see him by myself to get at the bottom of all this mystery.

I found my young count with Viar, who, judging by the awe the child shewed of me, must have thought he belonged to me. He was unsparing in his praises of his pupil, saying that he played the flute capitally, danced and fenced admirably, rode well, and wrote a good hand. He shewed me the pens he had cut himself with three, five, and even nine points, and begged to be examined on heraldry, which, as the master observed, was so necessary a science for a young nobleman.

The young gentleman then commenced in the jargon of heraldry to blazon his own pretended arms, and I felt much inclined to burst into laughter, partly because I did not understand a word he said, and partly because he seemed to think the matter as important as would a country squire with his thirty-two quarters. However, I was delighted to see his dexterity in penmanship, which was undoubtedly very great, and I expressed my satisfaction to Viar, who soon left us to ourselves. We proceeded into the garden.

"Will you kindly inform me," I said, "how you can be so foolish as to call yourself the Comte d'Aranda?"

He replied, with the utmost calmness, "I know it is foolish, but leave me my title; it is of service to me here and gains me respect."

"It is an imposition I cannot wink at, as it may be fraught with serious results, and may do harm to both of us. I should not have thought that at your age you would be capable of such a knavish trick. I know you did it out of stupidity, but after a certain limit stupidity becomes criminal; and I cannot see how I am to remedy your fault without disgracing you in the eyes of Madame d'Urfe."

I kept on scolding him till he burst into tears, saying,

"I had rather the shame of being sent back to my mother than the shame of confessing to Madame d'Urfe that I had imposed on her; and I could not bear to stay here if I had to give up my name."

Seeing that I could do nothing with him, unless, indeed, I sent him to some place far removed from Paris under his proper name, I told him to take comfort as I would try and do the best I could for both of us.

"And now tell me—and take care to tell the truth—what sort of feelings does Viar's daughter entertain for you?"

"I think, papa, that this is a case in which the reserve commended by yourself, as well as by mother, would be appropriate."

"Yes, that sort of answer tells me a good deal, but I think you are rather too knowing for your age. And you may as well observe that when you are called upon for a confession, reserve is out of place, and it's a confession I require from you."

"Well, papa, Viar's daughter is very fond of me, and she shews her love in all sorts of ways."

"And do you love her?"

"Oh, yes!"

"Is she much with you in the morning?"

"She is with me the whole day."

"She is present when you go to bed?"

"Yes, she helps me to undress."

"Nothing else?"

"I do not care to tell you."

I was astonished at the measured way in which he answered me, and as I had heard enough to guess that the boy and girl were very good friends indeed, I contented myself with warning him to take care of his health, and with this I left him.

Some time after, my thoughts were occupied with a business speculation which all my calculations assured me would be extremely profitable. The plan was to produce on silks, by means of printing, the exquisite designs which are produced at Lyons by the tedious process of weaving, and thus to give customers excellent value at much lower prices. I had the requisite knowledge of chemistry, and enough capital to make the thing a success. I obtained the assistance of a man with the necessary technical skill and knowledge, intending to make him my manager.

I told my plan to the Prince de Conti, who encouraged me to persevere, promising me his patronage, and all the privileges I could wish for. That decided me to begin.

I rented a very large house near the Temple for a thousand crowns per annum. The house contained a spacious hall, in which I meant to put my workmen; another hall which was to be the shop; numerous rooms for my workpeople to live in; and a nice room for myself in case I cared to live on the premises.

I made the scheme into a company with thirty shares, of which I gave five to my designer, keeping the remaining twenty-five to distribute to those who were inclined to join the company. I gave one to a doctor who, on giving surety, became the storekeeper, and came to live in the house with his whole family; and I engaged four servants, a waiting-maid, and a porter. I had to give another share to an accountant, who furnished me with two clerks, who also took up their abode in the house. The carpenters, blacksmiths, and painters worked hard from morning to night, and in less than three weeks the place was ready. I told the manager to engage twenty girls to paint, who were to be paid every Saturday. I stocked the warehouse with three hundred pieces of sarcenet and camlet of different shades and colours to receive the designs, and I paid for everything in ready money.

I had made an approximate calculation with my manager that I should have to spend three hundred thousand francs, and that would not break me. If the worst happened I could fall back on my shares, which produced a good income, but I hoped I should not be compelled to do so, as I wanted to have an income of two hundred thousand francs a year.

All the while I did not conceal from myself that the speculation might be my ruin, if custom did not come in, but on looking at my beautiful materials these fears were dispelled, especially as I heard everybody saying that I sold them much too cheap.

To set up the business I spent in the course of a month about sixty thousand francs, and my weekly expenses amounted to twelve hundred francs.

As for Madame d'Urfe she laughed every time she saw me, for she was quite certain that this business was only meant to put the curious off the scent and to preserve my incognito: so persuaded was she of my omnipotence.

The sight of twenty girls, all more or less pretty, the eldest of whom was not twenty-five, far from making me tremble as it ought, delighted me. I fancied myself in the midst of a seraglio, and I amused myself by watching their meek and modest looks as they did their work under the direction of the foreman. The best paid did not get more than twenty-four sous a day, and all of them had excellent reputations, for they had been selected at her own request by the manager's wife, a devout woman of ripe age, whom I hoped to find obliging if the fancy seized me to test her choice. Manon Baletti did not share my satisfaction in them. She trembled to see me the owner of a harem, well knowing that sooner or later the barque of my virtue would run on the rocks. She scolded me well about these girls, though I assured her that none of them slept in the house.

This business increased my own ideas of my importance; partly from the thought that I was on the high road to fortune, and partly because I furnished so many people with the means of subsistence. Alas! I was too fortunate; and my evil genius soon crossed my career.

It was now three months since Mdlle. X. C. V. had gone into the convent, and the time of her delivery drew near. We wrote to each other twice a week, and I considered the matter happily settled; M. de la Popeliniere had married, and when Mdlle. X. C. V. returned to her mother there would be nothing more to be said But just at this period, when my happiness seemed assured, the hidden fire leapt forth and threatened to consume me; how, the reader will see.

One day after leaving Madame d'Urfe's I went to walk in the Tuileries. I had taken a couple of turns in the chief walk when I saw that an old woman, accompanied by a man dressed in black, was looking at me closely and communicating her observations to her companion. There was nothing very astonishing in this in a public place, and I continued my walk, and on turning again saw the same couple still watching me. In my turn I looked at them, and remembered seeing the man in a gaming-house, where he was known by the name of Castel-Bajac. On scrutinizing the features of the hag, I at last succeeded in recollecting who she was; she was the woman to whom I had taken Mdlle. X. C. V. I felt certain that she had recognized me, but not troubling myself about the matter I left the gardens to walk elsewhere. The day after next, just as I was going to get into my carriage, a man of evil aspect gave me a paper and asked me to read it. I opened it, but finding it covered with an illegible scrawl I gave it him back, telling him to read it himself. He did so, and I found myself summoned to appear before the commissary of police to answer to the plea which the midwife (whose name I forget) brought against me.

Although I could guess what the charge would be, and was certain that the midwife could furnish no proofs of her accusation, I went to an attorney I knew and told him to appear for me. I instructed him that I did not know any midwife in Paris whatsoever. The attorney waited on the commissary, and on the day after brought me a copy of the pleas.

The midwife said that I came to her one night, accompanied by a young lady about five months with child, and that, holding a pistol in one hand and a packet of fifty Louis in the other, I made her promise to procure abortion. We both of us (so she said) had masks on, thus shewing that we had been at the opera ball. Fear, said she, had prevented her from flatly refusing to grant my request; but she had enough presence of mind to say that the necessary drugs were not ready, that she would have all in order by the next night; whereupon we left, promising to return. In the belief that we would not fail to keep the appointment, she went in to M. Castel-Bajac to ask him to hide in the next room that she might be protected from my fury, and that he might be a witness of what I said, but she had not seen me again. She added that she would have given information the day after the event if she had known who I was, but since M. Castel-Bajac had told her my name on her recognizing me in the Tuileries, she had thought it her bounden duty to deliver me to the law that she might be compensated for the violence I had used to her. And this document was signed by the said Castel-Bajac as a witness.

"This is an evident case of libel," said my attorney, "at least, if she can't prove the truth of her allegations. My advice to you is to take the matter before the criminal lieutenant, who will be able to give you the satisfaction you require."

I authorized him to do what he thought advisable, and three or four days after he told me that the lieutenant wished to speak to me in private, and would expect me the same day at three o'clock in the afternoon.

As will be expected, I was punctual to the appointment. I found the magistrate to be a polite and good-hearted gentleman. He was, in fact, the well-known M. de Sartine, who was the chief of police two years later. His office of criminal lieutenant was saleable, and M. de Sartine sold it when he was appointed head of the police.

As soon as I had made my bow, he asked me to sit down by him, and addressed me as follows:

"I have asked you to call upon me in the interests of both of us, as in your position our interests are inseparable. If you are innocent of the charge which has been brought against you, you are quite right to appeal to me; but before proceedings begin, you should tell me the whole truth. I am ready to forget my position as judge, and to give you my help, but you must see yourself that to prove the other side guilty of slander, you must prove yourself innocent. What I want from you is an informal and strictly confidential declaration, for the case against you is a serious one, and of such a kind as to require all your efforts to wipe off this blot upon your honour. Your enemies will not respect your delicacy of feeling. They will press you so hard that you will either be obliged to submit to a shameful sentence, or to wound your feelings of honour in proving your innocence. You see I am confiding in you, for in certain cases honour seems so precious a thing to me that I am ready to defend it with all the power of the law. Pay me back, then, in the same coin, trust in me entirely, tell me the whole story without any reserves, and you may rely upon my good offices. All will be well if you are innocent, for I shall not be the less a judge because I am your friend; but if you are guilty I am sorry for you, for I warn you that I shall be just."

After doing my best to express my gratitude to him, I said that my position did not oblige me to make any reservations on account of honour, and that I had, consequently, no informal statement to make him.

"The midwife," I added, "is absolutely unknown to me. She is most likely an abandoned woman, who with her worthy companion wants to cheat me of my money."

"I should be delighted to think so," he answered, "but admitting the fact, see how chance favours her, and makes it a most difficult thing for you to prove your innocence.

"The young lady disappeared three months ago. She was known to be your intimate friend, you called upon her at all hours; you spent a considerable time with her the day before she disappeared, and no one knows what has become of her; but everyone's suspicions point at you, and paid spies are continually dogging your steps. The midwife sent me a requisition yesterday by her counsel, Vauversin. She says that the pregnant lady you brought to her house is the same whom Madame X. C. V. is searching for. She also says that you both wore black dominoes, and the police have ascertained that you were both at the ball in black dominoes on the same night as that on which the midwife says you came to her house; you are also known to have left the ball-room together. All this, it is true, does not constitute full proof of your guilt, but it makes one tremble for your innocence."

"What cause have I to tremble?"

"What cause! Why a false witness, easily enough hired for a little money, might swear with impunity that he saw you come from the opera together; and a coachman in the same way might swear he had taken you to the midwife's. In that case I should be compelled to order your arrest and examination, with a view to ascertain the name of the person whom you took with you. Do you realize that you are accused of procuring abortion; that three months have gone by without the lady's retreat having been discovered; that she is said to be dead. Do you realize, in short, what a very serious charge murder is?"

"Certainly; but if I die innocent, you will have condemned me wrongly, and will be more to be pitied than I."

"Yes, yes, but that wouldn't make your case any better. You may be sure, however, that I will not condemn an innocent man; but I am afraid that you will be a long time in prison before you succeed in proving your innocence. To be brief, you see that in twenty-four hours the case looks very bad, and in the course of a week it might look very much worse. My interest was aroused in your favour by the evident absurdity of the accusations, but it is the other circumstances about the case which make it a serious one for you. I can partly understand the circumstances, and the feelings of love and honour which bid you be silent. I have spoken to you, and I hope you will have no reserves with me. I will spare you all the unpleasant circumstances which threaten you, believing, as I do, that you are innocent. Tell me all, and be sure that the lady's honour will not suffer; but if, on the other hand, you are unfortunately guilty of the crimes laid to your charge, I advise you to be prudent, and to take steps which it is not my business to suggest. I warn you that in three or four days I shall cite you to the bar of the court, and that you will then find in me only the judge—just, certainly, but severe and impartial."

I was petrified; for these words shewed me my danger in all its nakedness. I saw how I should esteem this worthy man's good offices, and said to him in quite another tone, that innocent as I was, I saw that my best course was to throw myself on his kindness respecting Mdlle. X. C. V., who had committed no crime, but would lose her reputation by this unhappy business.

"I know where she is," I added, "and I may tell you that she would never have left her mother if she had not endeavoured to force her into a marriage she abhorred."

"Well, but the man is now married; let her return to her mother's house, and you will be safe, unless the midwife persists in maintaining that you incited her to procure abortion."

"There is no abortion in the matter; but other reasons prevent her returning to her family. I can tell you no more without obtaining the consent of another party. If I succeed in doing so I shall be able to throw the desired light on the question. Be kind enough to give me a second hearing on the day after to-morrow."

"I understand. I shall be delighted to hear what you have to say. I thank and congratulate you. Farewell!"

I was on the brink of the precipice, but I was determined to leave the kingdom rather than betray the honour of my poor dear sweetheart. If it had been possible, I would gladly have put an end to the case with money; but it was too late. I was sure that Farsetti had the chief hand in all this trouble, that he was continually on my track, and that he paid the spies mentioned by M. de Sartine. He it was who had set Vauversin, the barrister, after me, and I had no doubt that he would do all in his power to ruin me.

I felt that my only course was to tell the whole story to M. de Sartine, but to do that I required Madame du Rumain's permission.

V

My Examination I Give the Clerk Three Hundred
Louis—The Midwife and Cartel-Bajac Imprisoned—Mdlle.
X. C. V. is Brought to Bed of a Son and Obliges Her
Mother to Make Me Amends—The Suit Against Me is
Quashed—Mdlle. X. C. V. Goes with Her Mother to
Brussels and from Thence to Venice, Where She Becomes
a Great Lady—My Work-girls—Madame Baret—I Am
Robbed, Put in Prison, and Set at Liberty Again—I Go
to Holland—Helvetius' "Esprit"—Piccolomini

The day after my interview with M. de Sartine I waited on Madame
du Rumain at an early hour. Considering the urgency of the case I
took the liberty of rousing her from her slumbers, and as soon as she was
ready to receive me I told her all.

"There can be no hesitation in the matter," said this delightful woman.
"We must make a confidant of M. de Sartine, and I will speak to him
myself to-day without fail."

Forthwith she went to her desk and wrote to the criminal lieutenant
asking him to see her at three o'clock in the afternoon. In less than
an hour the servant returned with a note in which he said he would
expect her. We agreed that I should come again in the evening, when
she would tell me the result of her interview.

I went to the house at five o'clock, and had only a few minutes to
wait.

"I have concealed nothing," said she; "he knows that she is on the eve
of her confinement, and that you are not the father, which speaks highly
for your generosity. I told him that as soon as the confinement was
over, and the young lady had recovered her health, she would return to
her mother, though she would make no confession, and that the child
should be well looked after. You have now nothing to fear, and can calm
yourself; but as the case must go on you will be cited before the court
the day after to-morrow. I advise you to see the clerk of the court on
some pretext or other, and to make him accept a sum of money."

I was summoned to appear, and I appeared. I saw M. de Sartine,
'sedentem pro tribunali'. At the end of the sitting he told me that he was
obliged to remand me, and that during my remand I must not leave Paris

or get married, as all my civil rights were in suspense pending the decision. I promised to follow his commands.

I acknowledged in my examination that I was at the ball in a black domino on the night named in my accusation, but I denied everything else. As for Mdlle. X. C. V., I said that neither I nor anyone of her family had any suspicion that she was with child.

Recollecting that I was an alien, and that this circumstance might make Vauversin call for my arrest, on the plea that I might fly the kingdom, I thought the moment opportune for making interest with the clerk of the court, and I accordingly paid him a visit. After telling him of my fears, I slipped into his hand a packet of three hundred louis, for which I did not ask for a receipt, saying that they were to defray expenses if I were mulcted in cósts. He advised me to require the midwife to give bail for her appearance, and I told my attorney to do so; but, four days after, the following incident took place:

I was walking in the Temple Gardens, when I was accosted by a Savoyard, who gave me a note in which I was informed that somebody in an alley, fifty paces off, wanted to speak to me. "Either a love affair or a challenge," I said to myself, "let's see." I stopped my carriage, which was following me, and went to the place.

I cannot say how surprised I was to see the wretched Cartel-Bajac standing before me. "I have only a word to say," said he, when he saw me. "We will not be overheard here. The midwife is quite sure that you are the man who brought a pregnant lady to her, but she is vexed that you are accused of making away with her. Give her a hundred louis; she will then declare to the court that she has been mistaken, and your trouble will be ended. You need not pay the money till she has made her declaration; we will take your word for it. Come with me and talk it over with Vauversin. I am sure he will persuade you to do as I suggest. I know where to find him, follow me at some distance."

I had listened to him in silence, and I was delighted to see that the rascals were betraying themselves. "Very good," said I to the fellow, "you go on, and I will follow." I went after him to the third floor of a house in the Rue aux Ours, where I found Vauversin the barrister. No sooner had I arrived than he went to business without any prefatory remarks.

"The midwife," he said, "will call on you with a witness apparently with the intention of maintaining to your face that you are her man; but she won't be able to recognize you. She will then proceed with the witness to the court, and will declare that she has made a mistake, and the criminal lieutenant will forthwith put an end to the proceedings. You will thus be certain of gaining your case against the lady's mother."

I thought the plan well conceived, and said that they would find me at the Temple any day up to noon.

"But the midwife wants a hundred louis badly."

"You mean that the worthy woman rates her perjury at that price. Well, never mind, I will pay the money, and you may trust to my word; but I can't do so before she has taken oath to her mistake before the court."

"Very good, but you must first give me twenty-five louis to reimburse me for my costs and fees."

"Certainly, if you will give me a formal receipt for the money."

He hesitated at first, but after talking it over the money proved too strong a bait, and he wrote out the receipt and I gave him the twenty-five louis. He thanked me, and said that though Madame X. C. V. was his client, he would let me know confidentially how best to put a stop to the proceedings. I thanked him with as much gratitude as if I had really intended to make use of his services, and I left to write and tell M. de Sartine what had taken place.

Three days afterwards I was told that a man and woman wanted to see me. I went down and asked the woman what she wanted.

"I want to speak to M. Casanova."

"I am he."

"Then I have made a mistake, for which I hope you will forgive me."

Her companion smiled, and they went off.

The same day Madame du Rumain had a letter from the abbess telling her that her young friend had given birth to a fine boy, who had been sent away to a place where he would be well looked after. She stated that the young lady could not leave the convent for the next six weeks, at the end of which time she could return to her mother with a certificate which would protect her from all annoyance.

Soon after the midwife was put in solitary confinement, Castel-Bajac was sent to The Bicetre, and Vauversin's name was struck off the rolls. The suit instituted against me by Madame X. C. V. went on till her daughter reappeared, but I knew that I had nothing to fear. The girl returned to her mother about the end of August armed with a certificate from the abbess, who said she had been under her protection for four months, during which time she had never left the convent or seen any persons from outside. This was perfectly true, but the abbess added that her only reason for her going back to her family was that she had nothing more to dread from the attentions of M. de la Popeliniere, and in this the abbess lied.

Mdlle. X. C. V. profited by the delight of her mother in seeing her again safe and sound, and made her wait on M. de Sartine with the abbess's certificate, stop all proceedings against me, and withdraw all the charges she had made. Her daughter told her that if I liked I might claim damages for libel, and that if she did not wish to injure her reputation she would say nothing more about what had happened.

The mother wrote me a letter of the most satisfactory character, which I had registered in court, thus putting an end to the prosecution. In my turn I wrote to congratulate her on the recovery of her daughter, but I never set foot in her house again, to avoid any disagreeable scenes with Farsetti.

Mdlle. X. C. V. could not stay any longer in Paris, where her tale was known to everyone, and Farsetti took her to Brussels with her sister Madelaine. Some time after, her mother followed her, and they then went on to Venice, and there in three years' time she became a great lady. Fifteen years afterwards I saw her again, and she was a widow, happy enough apparently, and enjoying a great reputation on account of her rank, wit, and social qualities, but our connection was never renewed.

In four years the reader will hear more of Castel-Bajac. Towards the end of the same year (1759), before I went to Holland, I spent several hundred francs to obtain the release of the midwife.

I lived like a prince, and men might have thought me happy, but I was not. The enormous expenses I incurred, my love of spending money, and magnificent pleasures, warned me, in spite of myself, that there were rocks ahead. My business would have kept me going for a long time, if custom had not been paralyzed by the war; but as it was, I, like everybody else, experienced the effect of bad times. My warehouse contained four hundred pieces of stuffs with designs on them, but as I could not hope to dispose of them before the peace, and as peace seemed a long way off, I was threatened with ruin.

With this fear I wrote to Esther to get her father to give me the remainder of my money, to send me a sharp clerk, and to join in my speculation. M. d'O—— said that if I would set up in Holland he would become responsible for everything and give me half profits, but I liked Paris too well to agree to so good an offer. I was sorry for it afterwards.

I spent a good deal of money at my private house, but the chief expense of my life, which was unknown to others but which was ruining me, was incurred in connection with the girls who worked in my establishment. With my complexion and my pronounced liking for variety, a score of girls, nearly all of them pretty and seductive, as most Paris girls are, was a reef on which my virtue made shipwreck every day. Curiosity had a good deal to do with it, and they profited by my impatience to take possession by selling their favours dearly. They all followed the example of the first favourite, and everyone claimed in turn an establishment, furniture, money, and jewels; and I knew too little of the value of money to care how much they asked. My fancy never lasted longer than a week, and often waned in three or four days, and the last comer always appeared the most worthy of my attentions.

As soon as I had made a new choice I saw no more of my old loves, but I continued to provide for them, and that with a good deal of money. Madame d'Urfe, who thought I was rich, gave me no trouble. I made her happy by using my oracle to second the magical ceremonies of which she grew fonder every day, although she never attained her aim. Manon Baletti, however, grieved me sorely by her jealousy and her well-founded reproaches. She would not understand—and I did not wonder at it—how I could put off marrying her if I really loved her. She accused me of deceiving her. Her mother died of consumption in our arms. Silvia had won my true friendship. I looked upon her as a most worthy woman, whose kindness of heart and purity of life deserved the esteem of all. I stayed in the family for three days after her death, sincerely sympathizing with them in their affliction.

A few days afterwards, my friend Tiretta lost his mistress through a grievous illness. Four days before her death, perceiving that she was near her end, she willed to consecrate to God that which man could have no longer, and dismissed her lover with the gift of a valuable jewel and a purse of two hundred louis. Tiretta marched off and came and told me the sad news. I got him a lodging near the Temple, and a month after, approving his idea to try his fortune in India, I gave him a letter of introduction to M. d'O——, of Amsterdam; and in the course of a week this gentleman got him a post as clerk, and shipped him aboard one of the company's ships which was bound for Batavia. If he had behaved well he might have become a rich man, but he got involved in some conspiracy and had to fly, and afterwards experienced many vicissitudes of fortune. I heard from one of his relations that he was in Bengal in 1788, in good circumstances, but unable to realize his property and so return to his native country. I do not know what became of him eventually.

In the beginning of November an official belonging to the Duc d'Elbeuf's household came to my establishment to buy a wedding dress for his daughter. I was dazzled with her beauty. She chose a fine satin, and her pretty face lighted up when she heard her father say he did not think it was too much; but she looked quite piteous when she heard the clerk tell her father that he would have to buy the whole piece, as they could not cut it. I felt that I must give in, and to avoid making an exception in her favour I beat a hasty retreat into my private room. I wish I had gone out of the house, as I should have saved a good deal of money; but what pleasure should I have also lost! In her despair the charming girl begged the manager to take her to me, and he dared not refuse to do so. She came in; two big tears falling down her cheeks and dimming the ardour of her gaze.

"Oh, sir!" she began, "you are rich, do you buy the piece and let me have enough for a dress, which will make me happy."

I looked at her father and saw he wore an apologetic air, as if deprecating the boldness of his child.

"I like your simplicity," I said to her, "and since it will make you happy, you shall have the dress."

She ran up to me, threw her arms round my neck and kissed me, while her worthy father was dying with laughter. Her kisses put the last stroke to my bewitchment. After he had paid for the dress, her father said,

"I am going to get this little madcap married next Sunday; there will be a supper and a ball, and we shall be delighted if you will honour us with your presence. My name is Gilbert. I am comptroller of the Duc d'Elbeuf's household."

I promised to be at the wedding, and the young lady gave a skip of joy which made me think her prettier than ever.

On Sunday I repaired to the house, but I could neither eat nor drink. The fair Mdlle. Gilbert kept me in a kind of enchantment which lasted while I was in company with her friends, for whom I did not care. They were all officials in noblemen's houses, with their wives and daughters, who all aped the manners of their betters in the most ridiculous way; nobody knew me and I was known to nobody, and I cut a sorry figure amongst them all, for in a company of this sort the wittiest man is the greatest fool. Everybody cracked his joke to the bride, she answered everybody, and people laughed at nothing.

Her husband, a thin and melancholy man, with a rather foolish expression, was delighted at his wife's keeping everybody amused. Although I was in love with her, I pitied rather than envied him. I guessed that he had married for monetary considerations, and I knew pretty well what kind of a head-dress his handsome, fiery wife would give her husband, who was plain-featured, and seemed not to be aware of his wife's beauty. I was seized with the desire of asking her some questions, and she gave me the opportunity by coming to sit next to me after a quadrille. She thanked me again for my kindness, and said that the beautiful dress I had supplied had won her many compliments.

"All the same," I said, "I know you are longing to take it off. I know what love is and how impatient it makes one."

"It's very funny that everyone persists in thinking that I am in love, though I saw M. Baret for the first time only a week ago. Before then I was absolutely unconscious of his existence."

"But why are you getting married in such a hurry without waiting till you know him better?"

"Because my father does everything in a hurry."

"I suppose your husband is a very rich man?"

"No, but he may become rich. We are going to open a shop for silk stockings at the corner of the Rue St. Honore and the Rue des Prouveres, and I hope that you will deal with us, as we would serve you with the best."

"I shall certainly do so—nay, I will be your first customer, if I have to wait at the door."

"You are kind! M. Baret," said she to her husband, who was standing close by, "this gentleman promises to be our first customer."

"The gentleman is very good," said the husband, "and I am sure he will be satisfied, as my stockings are genuine silk."

Next Tuesday at day-break I began to dance attendance at the corner of the Rue des Prouveres, and waited there till the servant came out to take down the shutters. I went in and the girl asked me my business.

"I want to buy some stockings," was my answer.

"Master and mistress are still in bed, so you had better come later on."

"No, I will wait here. Stop a minute," said I, giving her six francs, "go and get me some coffee; I will drink it in the shop."

"I might go and get you some coffee, but I am not so silly as to leave you in the shop by yourself."

"You are afraid I might steal something!"

"Well, one does hear of such things being done, and I don't know you from Adam."

"Very good; but I shall stay here all the same."

Before long Baret came down and scolded the poor girl for not having told him of my presence. "Go and tell my wife to come," said he, as he began opening packets of stockings for me to choose from. He kept stockings, vests, and silk drawers, and I turned one packet over after another, looking at them all and not fixing on anything till I saw his wife coming down as fresh as a rose and as bright as a lily. She smiled at me in the most seductive manner, apologized for the disorder of her dress, and thanked me for keeping my word.

"I never break my word," I said, "especially when such a charming lady is concerned!"

Madame Baret was seventeen, of a moderate height, and an exquisite figure; without being classically beautiful, a Raphael could not wish to depict a more enticing face. Her eyes were large and brilliant. Her drooping eyelids, which gave her so modest and yet so voluptuous an appearance, the ever-smiling mouth, her splendid teeth, the dazzling whiteness of her complexion, the pleasing air with which she listened to what was being said, her silvery voice, the sweetness and sparkling vivacity of her manner, her lack of conceit, or rather her unconsciousness of the power of her charms-in fine, everything about this masterpiece of nature made me wonder and admire; while she, by chance or vile monetary considerations, was in the power of Baret, who, pale and sickly, thought a good deal more of his stockings than of the treasure marriage had given him—a treasure of which he was all unworthy, since he could not see its beauty nor taste its sweetness.

I chose stockings and vests to the amount of twenty-five louis, and I paid the price without trying to cheapen them. I saw the face of the fair shopwoman light up, and I augured well for my success, though I could not expect to do much while the honeymoon lasted. I told the servant that I would give her six francs if she would bring the packet to my house, and so I left them.

Next Sunday Baret came himself with my purchases. I gave him six francs to hand over to his servant, but he hinted that he was not too proud to keep them himself. I was disgusted at this petty greed, and at his meanness in depriving his maid of the six francs after having made a good profit in what he had sold me; but I wanted to stand well with him, and I was not sorry to find so simple a way of throwing dust into his eyes. So while I resolved that the servant should not be a loser I gave the husband a good reception that I might the better mould him to my purpose. I had breakfast brought to him, asking why he had not brought his wife.

"She wanted me to take her," said he, "but I was afraid you might be offended."

"Not at all, I should have been delighted. I think your wife a charming woman."

"You are very kind to say so; but she's young, she's young."

"I don't think that's any objection; and if she cares for the walk, bring her with you another time." He said he should be very pleased to do so.

When I passed by the shop in my carriage I blew kisses to her with my hand, but I did not stop as I did not want any more stockings. Indeed, I should have been bored with the crowd of fops with which the shop was always full. She began to be a topic of conversation in the town; the Palais Royal was full of her; and I was glad to hear that she kept to herself as if she had richer prey in view. That told me that no one possessed her so far, and I hoped that I might be the prey myself; I was quite willing to be captured.

Some days after, she saw my carriage coming, and beckoned to me as I passed. I got out, and her husband with many apologies told me that he wanted me to be the first to see a new fashion in breeches he had just got in. The breeches were parti-coloured, and no man of fashion would be seen without them. They were odd-looking things, but became a well-made young man. As they had to fit exactly, I told him to measure me for six pairs, offering to pay in advance. "We have them in all sizes," said he, "go up to my wife's room and try some on."

It was a good opportunity and I accepted, especially when I heard him tell his wife to go and help me. I went upstairs, she following, and I began to undress, apologizing for doing so before her.

"I will fancy I am your valet," said she, "and I will help you."

I did not make any difficulties, and after taking off my shoes I gave her my breeches, taking care, however, to keep on my drawers, lest her modesty should receive too severe a shock. This done she took a pair of breeches, drew them on me, took them off, and tried on others, and all this without any impropriety on either side; for I had determined to behave with discretion till the opportunity came to be indiscreet. She decided that four pairs fitted me admirably, and, not wishing to contradict her, I gave her the sixteen louis she asked, and told her I should be delighted if she would bring them herself at any time when she was at leisure. She came downstairs quite proud of her knowledge of business, and Baret said that next Sunday he and his wife would have the honour of bringing me my purchase.

"I shall be charmed, M. Baret," said I, "especially if you will stay to dinner."

He answered that having an important engagement for two o'clock he could only accept on the condition that I would let him go at that time, and he would return at about five to fetch his wife. I found the plan vastly to my taste, but I knew how to conceal my joy; and I quietly said that though I should lose the pleasure of his society, he was free to go when he liked, especially as I had not to go out myself before six.

I looked forward to the Sunday, and the tradesman and his wife did not fail me. As soon as they arrived, I told my servant to say "Not at home" for the rest of the day, and as I was impatient to know what would happen in the afternoon I had dinner served at an early hour. The dishes were exquisite, and the wines delicious. The good man ate much and drank deeply, indeed to such an extent that in common politeness I was obliged to remind him that he had an important appointment at two. His wits being sharpened with champagne, the happy thought occurred to him to tell his wife to go home by herself, if he were kept later than five; and I hastened to add that I would take her home myself in my carriage. He thanked me, and I soothed his uneasiness about being punctual to his appointment by telling him that a coach was waiting, and that the fare had been paid. He went off, and I found myself alone with my jewel, whom I was certain of possessing till six o'clock.

As soon as I heard the hall door shut on the kind husband, I said to his wife,

"You are to be congratulated on having such a kind husband; with a man like that your happiness is assured."

"It is easy to say happiness, but enjoying it is a different thing. My husband's health is so delicate that I can only consider myself as his nurse; and then he contracted heavy debts to set up in business which oblige us to observe the strictest economy. We came here on foot to save the twenty-four sons. We could live on the profits of the business, if there were no debts, but as it is everything goes to pay the interest, and our sales are not large enough to cover everything."

"But you have plenty of customers, for whenever I pass I see the shop full of people."

"These customers you see are idlers, crackers of bad jokes, and profligates, who come and make my head ache with their jests. They have not a penny to bless themselves with, and we dare not let them out of our sight for fear of their hands wandering. If we had cared to give them credit, our shop would have been emptied long ago. I am rude to them, in the hopes that they may leave me alone, but it's of no use. Their impudence is astonishing. When my husband is in I retreat to my room, but he is often away, and then I am obliged to put up with them. And the scarcity of money prevents us from doing much business, but we are obliged to pay our workmen all the same. As far as I can see, we shall be obliged to dismiss them, as we shall soon have to meet several bills. Next Saturday we have got to pay six hundred francs, and we have only got two hundred."

"I am surprised at your having all this worry in these early days of your marriage. I suppose your father knew about your husband's circumstances; how about your dowry?"

"My dowry of six thousand francs has served, most of it, to stock the shop and to pay our debts. We have goods which would pay our debts three times over; but in bad times capital sunk is capital dead."

"I am sorry to hear all this, as if peace is not made your situation will become worse, for as you go on your needs will become greater."

"Yes, for when my husband is better we may have children."

"What! Do you mean to say his health prevents him from making you a mother? I can't believe it."

"I don't see how I can be a mother who am still a maid; not that I care much about the matter."

"I shouldn't have believed it! How can a man not in the agony of death feel ill beside you? He must be dead."

"Well, he is not exactly dead, but he doesn't shew many signs of life."

This piece of wit made me laugh, and under cover of my applause I embraced her without experiencing much resistance. The first kiss was like an electric spark; it fired my imagination and I increased my attentions till she became as submissive as a lamb.

"I will help you, dearest, to meet the bill on Saturday;" and so saying I drew her gently into a closet where a soft divan formed a suitable altar for the completion of an amorous sacrifice.

I was enchanted to find her submissive to my caresses and my inquisitiveness, but she surprised me greatly when, as I placed myself in readiness for the consummation of the act, and was already in the proper posture between the two columns, she moved in such a way as to hinder my advance. I thought at first that it was only one of those devices intended to make the final victory more sweet by putting difficulties in the way; but, finding that her resistance was genuine, I exclaimed,

"How was I to expect a refusal like this at a moment when I thought I saw my ardours reflected in your eyes?"

"Your eyes did not deceive you; but what would my husband say if he found me otherwise than as God has made me?"

"He can't have left you untouched!"

"He really has done so. You can see for yourself if you like. Can I, then, give to you what appertains to the genius of the marriage-bed."

"You are right, my angel; this fruit must be kept for a mouth unworthy to taste it. I pity and adore you. Come to my arms, abandon yourself to my love, and fear nothing. The fruit shall not be damaged; I will but taste the outer surface and leave no trace behind."

We passed three hours in trifling together in a manner calculated to inflame our passions despite the libations which we now and again poured forth. I was consoled by her swearing to be mine as soon as Baret had good grounds for thinking that she was his, and, after taking her on the Boulevards, I left her at her door, with a present of twenty-five Louis.

I was in love with her as I had never been before, and I passed the shop three or four times a day, going round and round, to the wrath of my coachman, who got sick of telling me that I was ruining my horses. I was happy to see her watch for the moment that I passed, and waft me a kiss by putting her pretty fingers to her mouth.

We had agreed that she should not make me a sign to leave my coach till her husband had forced a passage. At last this day, so ardently desired and so long waited for, arrived. The sign was given, and I stopped the coach and she came out and, standing on the step, told me to go and wait for her at the church door of St. Germain l'Auxerrois.

I was curious to know what the results would be, and had not been at the place appointed more than a quarter of an hour when she came towards me, her head muffled in a hood. She got into the carriage and, saying that she wanted to make some purchases, begged me to take her to the shops.

I had business of my own, and pressing business too, but who can refuse the Beloved Object anything? I told the coachman to drive to the Place Dauphine, and I prepared to loosen my purse-strings, as I had a feeling she was going to treat me as a friend. In point of fact she left few shops unvisited, going from jewels to pretty trifles and toys of different kinds, and from these to dresses of the latest fashion, which they displayed before her, addressing her as princess, and saying that this would become her admirably. She looked at me, and said it must be confessed that it was very pretty and that she would like it if it were not so dear. I was a willing dupe, and assured her that if she liked it it could not be too dear, and that I would pay.

While my sweetheart was thus choosing one trifle after another my ill-luck brought about an incident which placed me in a fearful situation four years afterwards. The chain of events is endless.

I perceived at my left hand a pretty girl of twelve or thirteen, with an old and ugly woman who was disparaging a pair of ear-rings which the girl had in her hands, and on which she had evidently set her heart: she looked sad at not being able to buy them. I heard her say to the old woman that they would make her happy, but she snatched them from the girl's hands and told her to, come away.

"I can let you have a cheaper pair and almost as fine," said the shopwoman, but the young lady said she did not; care about it, and was getting ready to go, making a profound reverence to my princess Baret.

She, no doubt flattered by this sign of respect went up to her, called her little queen, told her she was as fair as a May morning, and asked the old woman her name,

"She is Mdlle. de Boulainvilier, my niece."

"How can you be so hard-hearted," said I to the aunt, "as to refuse your charming niece a toy which would make her happy? Allow me to make her a present of them."

So saying I put the ear-rings in the girl's hands, while she blushed and looked at her aunt as if to ask her permission.

"You may have the ear-rings," said she, "as this gentleman has been kind enough to give you such a present, and you should give him a kiss by way of thanks."

"The ear-rings," said the shopwoman, "will be only three louis."

Hereupon the affair took a comic turn; the old woman got into a rage and said,

"How can you be such a cheat? You told me they were only two louis."

"Nay, madam, I asked three."

"That's a lie, and I shall not allow you to rob this gentleman. Niece, put those ear-rings down; let the shopwoman keep them."

So far all was well enough; but the old aunt spoilt everything by saying that if I liked to give her niece the three louis she could get her a pair twice as good at another shop. It was all the same to me, so I smilingly put the three louis in front of the young lady, who still had the ear-rings in her hands. The shop-woman, who was on the look-out, pocketed the money, saying that the bargain was made, that the three louis belonged to her and the ear-rings to the young lady.

"You are a cheat," cried out the enraged old woman.

"And you are an old b——d," answered the shop-woman, "I know you well." A crowd began to gather in front of the shop, hearing the cries of the two harpies. Foreseeing a good deal of unpleasantness, I took the aunt by the arm and led her gently away. The niece, who was quite content with the ear-rings, and did not care whether they cost three louis or two, followed her. We shall hear of them again in due course.

My dear Baret having made me waste a score of louis, which her poor husband would have regretted much more than myself, we got into the carriage again, and I took her to the church door from which we had started. On the way she told me she was coming to stop a few days with me at Little Poland, and that it was her husband who would ask me for the invitation.

"When will he do that?"

"To-morrow, if you go by the shop. Come and buy some stockings; I shall have a bad headache, and Baret will speak to you."

It may be imagined that I took care to call the next day, and as I did not see his wife in the shop I asked in a friendly way after her health.

"She is ill in bed," he replied; "she wants a little country air."

"If you have not fixed for any place, I shall be happy to put you up at Little Poland."

He replied by a smile of delight.

"I will go and urge her to come myself; in the meanwhile, M. Baret, will you pack me up a dozen pairs of stockings?"

I went upstairs and found the invalid in bed, and laughing in spite of her imaginary headache. "The business is done," said I, "you will soon hear of it." As I had said, the husband came upstairs with my stockings and told her that I had been good enough to give her a room in my house. The crafty little creature thanked me, assuring her husband that the fresh air would soon cure her.

"You shall be well looked after," said I, "but you must excuse me if I do not keep you company—I have to attend to my business. M. Baret will be able to come and sleep with you every night, and start early enough in the morning to be in time for the opening of his shop."

After many compliments had been interchanged, Baret decided on having his sister stay in the house while his wife was away, and as I took leave I said that, I should give orders for their reception that very evening, in case I was out when they came.

Next day I stayed out till after midnight, and the cook told me that the wedded couple had made a good supper and had gone to bed. I warned her that I should be dining at home every day, and that I should not see my company.

The following day I was up betimes, and on enquiring if the husband had risen I learnt that he had got up at day-break and would not be back till supper-time. The wife was still asleep. I thought with reason she was not asleep for me, and I went to pay her my first visit. In point of fact she was awake, and I took a foretaste of greater joys by a thousand kisses, which she returned with interest. We jested at the expense of the worthy man who had trusted me with a jewel of which I was about to make such good use, and we congratulated each other on the prospect of a week's mutual pleasures.

"Come, my dear," said I, "get up and put on a few clothes and we will take breakfast in my room."

She did not make an elaborate toilette; a cotton dressing gown, a pretty lace cap, a lawn kerchief, that was all, but how the simple dress was lighted by the roses of her cheeks! We were quick over our breakfast, we were in a hurry, and when we had done I shut the door and we gave ourselves over to the enjoyment of our bliss.

Surprised to find her in the same condition in which I had left her, I told her I had hoped. . . but she, without giving me time to finish the phrase, said,

"My jewel, Baret thinks, or pretends to think, that he has done his duty as a husband; but he is no hand at the business, and I am disposed to put myself in your hands, and then there will be no doubt of my condition."

"We shall thus, my sweet, be doing him a service, and the service shall be well done."

As I said these words I was on the threshold of the temple, and I opened the door in a manner that overthrew all obstacles. A little scream and then several sighs announced the completion of the sacrifice, and, to tell the truth, the altar of love was covered with the blood of the victim. After the necessary ablutions the priest once more began his pious work, while the victim growing bolder so provoked his rage that it was not till the fourth mactation that we rested and put off our joust to another season. We swore a thousand times to love each other and to remain constant, and we may possibly have been sincere, as we were in our ecstasy of pleasure.

We only separated to dress; then after taking a turn in the garden we dined together, sure that in a sumptuous repast, washed down by the choicest wines, we should find strength to reanimate our desires and to lull them to sleep in bliss.

At dessert, as I was pouring champagne into her glass, I asked her how with such a fiery temperament she had managed to preserve her virtue?

"Cupid," said I, "might have gathered the fruit that Hymen could not taste. You are seventeen, and the pear has been ripe for two years at least."

"Very true, but I have never had a lover."

"Never?"

"I have been courted, but to no effect. My heart was ever silent. Possibly my father thought otherwise when I begged him, a month ago, to get me married soon."

"Very likely, but as you were not in love, why were you in such a hurry?"

"I knew that the Duc d'Elbeuf would soon be coming to town, and that if he found me still single he would oblige me to become the wife of a man I detest, who would have me at any price."

"Who is this man for whom you have such an aversion?"

"He is one of the duke's pets, a monster who sleeps with his master."

"Really! I did not know the duke had such tastes."

"Oh yes; he is eighty-four, and he thinks himself a woman; he says he must have a husband."

"That is very funny. And is this aspirant to your hand a handsome man?"

"I think him horrible; but everybody else thinks he is a fine man."

The charming Baret spent a week with me, and each day we renewed the combat in which we were always conquerors and always conquered.

I have seen few women as pretty and seductive, and none whose skin was more exquisitely soft and fair. Her breath was aromatic, and this made her kisses most sweet. Her neck was exquisitely shaped, and the two globes, tipped with coral, were as hard as marble. The exquisite curves of her figure would have defied the skill of the ablest painter. I experienced an ineffable joy in contemplating her, and in the midst of my happiness I called myself unhappy because I could not satisfy all the desires which her charms aroused in me. The frieze which crowned her columns was composed of links of pale gold of the utmost fineness, and my fingers strove in vain to give them another direction to that which nature had given them. She could easily have been taught those lively yet graceful movements which double the pleasure; nature had done her part in that direction, and I do not think a more expert mistress in the art of love could be found.

Each of us looked forward to the day of her departure with equal grief, and our only consolation lay in the hope of meeting again, and often. Three days after she went away, I went to see her, more in love than ever, and I gave her two notes of five thousand francs apiece. Her husband might have his suspicions, but he was too happy at being enabled to pay his debts and to keep his shop open to say anything unpleasant. Many husbands besides himself think themselves lucky to have such productive wives.

In the beginning of November I sold shares for fifty thousand francs to a man named Gamier, living in the Rue du Mail, giving up to him a third part of the materials in my warehouse, and accepting a manager chosen by him and paid by the company. Three days after signing the deed I received the money; but in the night the doctor, my warehouseman, emptied the till and absconded. I have always thought that this robbery could not have been effected without the connivance of the painter. This loss was a serious blow to me, as my affairs were getting into an embroiled condition; and, for a finishing touch to my misfortunes, Gamier had me served with a summons to repay him the fifty thousand francs. My answer was that I was not liable, that his manager had been appointed, the agreement and sale of the shares was valid, and that he being one of the company would have to share in the loss. As he persisted in his claim, I was advised to go to law, but Gamier declared the agreement null and void, accusing me in an indirect manner of having appropriated the money which I had said was stolen. I would willingly have given him a good thrashing, but he was an old man, and that course would not have mended matters, so I kept my temper. The merchant who had given surety for the doctor was not to be found; he had become bankrupt. Garnier had all my stock seized, and sequestrated my horses, carriages, and all my private property.

While these troubles were harassing me, I dismissed all my work-girls, who had always been a great expense, and replaced them with workmen and some of my servants. The painter still retained his position, which was an assured one, as he always paid himself out of the sales.

My attorney was an honest man—a rare bird amongst lawyers—but my counsel, who kept telling me that the case would soon be decided, was a rascal. While the decision was pending, Garnier served me with a writ to pay the sum claimed. I took it to my counsel, who promised to appeal the same day, which he did not do, while he appropriated to his own use the money assigned by me for the costs of an action which, if there had been justice in France, I should certainly have gained. Two other summonses were issued against me, and before I knew what was going on a warrant was issued for my arrest. I was seized at eight o'clock in the morning, as I was driving along the Rue St. Denis. The sergeant of police sat beside me, a second got up beside the coachman, and a third stationed himself at the back of the coach, and in this state we drove to Fort l'Eveque.

As soon as the police had handed me over to the gaoler, he informed me that by payment of the fifty thousand francs, or by giving good bail, I might instantly regain my freedom.

"For the moment," said I, "I can neither command money nor bail."

"Very good, then you will stay in prison."

The gaoler took me to a decent-looking room, and I told him I had only been served with one writ.

"Very likely," answered he, "it often happens like that; but it is rather difficult to prove."

"Bring me writing materials, and have a trusty messenger at my disposal."

I wrote to my counsel, my attorney, to Madame d'Urfe, and to all my friends, including my brother, who was just married. The attorney called immediately, but the barrister contented himself with writing to the effect that as he had put in an appeal my seizure was illegal, and that damages might be recovered. He ended by begging me to give him a free hand, and to have patience for a few days.

Manon Baletti sent her brother with her diamond earrings. Madame du Rumain dispatched her barrister—a man of rare honesty— to me, and wrote a friendly note in which she said that if I wanted five hundred louis I should have them to-morrow. My brother neither wrote nor came to see me. As to dear Madame d'Urfe she sent to say that she would expect me at dinner. I thought she had gone mad, as I could not think she was making fun of me.

At eleven o'clock my room was full of people. Poor Baret had come weeping, and offering me all his shop held. I was touched by the worthy man's kindness. At last I was told that a lady in a coach wanted to see me. I waited, but nobody came. In my impatience I called the turnkey, who told me that, after questioning the clerk of the prison, she had gone away again. From the description I was given I had no difficulty in identifying the lady with Madame d'Urfe.

To find myself deprived of my liberty was a disagreeable shock to me. I thought of The Leads, and though my present situation was not to be compared with that, I cursed my fate as I foresaw that my imprisonment would damage my reputation. I had thirty thousand francs in hard cash and jewels to more than double that amount, but I could not decide on making such a sacrifice, in spite of the advice given by Madame du Rumain's barrister, who would have me got out of prison at any cost.

"All you have to do," said the barrister, "is to deposit half the sum demanded which I will give to the clerk of the court, and in a short time I can promise a decision in your favour and the restoration of your money."

We were discussing the matter, when the gaoler entered, and said, very politely,

"Sir, you are a free man again, and a lady is waiting for you at the door in her carriage."

I called Le Duc, my man, and told him to go and see who the lady was. He returned with the information that it was Madame d'Urfe. I made my bow to everybody, and after four very disagreeable hours of imprisonment, I found myself free again and sitting in a splendid coach.

Madame d'Urfe received me with dignified kindness, and a judge who was in the carriage apologized for his country, where strangers were exposed to such insults. I thanked Madame d'Urfe in a few words, telling her that I was glad to become her debtor, but that it was Garnier who benefited by her generosity. She replied with a pleasant smile that she was not so sure of that, and that we would talk it over at dinner.

She wanted me to go and walk in the Tuileries and the Palais Royal, to convince people that the report of my imprisonment had been false. I thought the advice excellent, and as I set out I promised to be with her at two o'clock.

After skewing myself at the two principal walks of Paris, amusing myself by the astonishment depicted on certain faces well known to me, I went and returned the ear-rings to my dear Manon, who gave an astonished but a happy cry when she saw me. I thanked her tenderly for the proof she had given me of her attachment, and said that I had been arrested by a plot for which I would make the plotters pay dear. After promising to spend the evening with them I went to Madame d'Urfe's.

This good lady, whose foible is well known to my readers, made me laugh when she said that her genius had told her that I had got myself arrested to be talked about, for reasons which were known only to myself.

"As soon as I was informed of your arrest," said she, "I went to the Fort l'Eveque, and on learning from the clerk what the affair was about, I deposited bonds to bail you out. If you are not in a position to have justice done you, Gamier will have to reckon with me before he takes the money I have deposited. But your first step should be to commence a criminal prosecution against your counsel, who has not only failed to put in your appeal but has robbed and deceived you."

I left her in the evening, assuring her that in a few days her bail should be returned to her; and went to the French and Italian plays in succession, taking care to render myself conspicuous that my reappearance might be complete. Afterwards I went to sup with Manon Baletti, who was too happy to have had an opportunity of spewing her affection for me; and her joy was full when I told her that I was going to give up business, for she thought that my seraglio was the only obstacle to my marriage with her.

The next day was passed with Madame du Rumain. I felt that my obligations to her were great, while she, in the goodness of her heart, was persuaded that she could make no adequate return to me for the oracles with which I furnished her, and by following which she was safely guided through the perplexities of life. I cannot understand how she, whose wit was keen, and whose judgment on other subjects was of the soundest kind, could be liable to such folly. I was sorry when I reflected that I could not undeceive her, and glad when I reflected that to this deceit of mine the kindness she had shewn me was chiefly due.

My imprisonment disgusted me with Paris, and made me conceive a hatred of the law, which I feel now. I found myself entangled in a double maze of knavery—Garnier was my foe, and so was my own counsel. Every time I went to plead, to spend my money amongst lawyers, and to waste the time better given to pleasure, I felt as if I was going to execution. In this perturbed kind of life, so contrary to my inclinations, I resolved to set to work in earnest to make my fortune, so that I might become independent and free to enjoy life according to my tastes. I decided in the first place that I would cut myself free of all that bound me to Paris, make a second journey into Holland to replenish my purse and invest my money in a yearly income for two lives, and from thenceforth live free from care. The two lives were those of my wife and myself; my wife would be Manon Baletti, and when I told her my plans she would have thought them delightful if I had begun by marrying her.

The first thing I did was to give up Little Poland. I then drew the twenty-four thousand francs which were my surety for keeping a lottery office in the Rue St. Denis. Thus I got rid of my ridiculous office of lottery receiver, and after getting my clerk married I handed over the office to him; in short, I made his fortune. A friend of his wife's was his surety; such things often happen.

I did not like to leave Madame d'Urfe involved in a troublesome suit with Gamier, so I went to Versailles to see the Abbe de la Ville, a great friend of his, and begged him to induce Gamier to make a composition.

The abbe saw that his friend was in the wrong, and so was all the more willing to help me; and a few days afterwards he wrote to me to go and see him, assuring me that I should find him inclined to arrange matters in a friendly manner.

Gamier was at Ruelle, where he had a house which cost him four hundred thousand francs—a fine estate for a man who had made his money as an army contractor during the last war. He was rich, but he was so unfortunate as to be still fond of women at the age of seventy, while his impotence debarred him from the proper enjoyment of their society. I found him in company with three young ladies, all of whom were pretty, and (as I heard afterwards) of good families; but they were poor, and their necessities forced them to submit to a disgusting intercourse with the old profligate. I stayed to dinner and admired the propriety and modesty of their behaviour in spite of the humiliation which accompanies poverty. After dinner, Gamier went to sleep, and left me to entertain these girls whom I would willingly have rescued from their unfortunate situation if I had been able. After Gamier woke, we went into his study to talk over our business.

At first he maintained his claim tenaciously, and seemed unwilling to yield an inch; but when I told him that I was leaving Paris in a few days, he saw that as he could not keep me, Madame d'Urfe might take the suit over and carry it on to infinity, and that he might lose it at last. That made him think it over, and he asked me to stay in his house for the night. The next day, after breakfast, he said,—

"I have made up my mind: I will have twenty-five thousand francs, or keep the matter before the courts till my dying day."

I answered that he would find the sum in the hands of Madame d'Urfe's solicitor, and that he could receive it as soon as he had given replevy on the bail at the Fort l'Eveque.

I could not persuade Madame d'Urfe that I had acted wisely in coming to an arrangement till I had told her that my genius had commanded me not to leave Paris before my affairs were settled, so that no one might be able to accuse me of having gone away to avoid creditors whose claims I could not satisfy.

Three or four days afterwards I went to take leave of M. de Choiseul, who promised to instruct M. d'Afri to aid me in negotiating a loan at five per cent. either with the States-General or a private company.

"You can tell everyone," said he, "that peace is certain to be made in the course of the winter, and I will take care that you shall have what is due to you on your return to France."

M. de Choiseul deceived me, for he knew very well that peace would not be made; but I had no definite project, and I repented of having given M. de Boulogne my confidence, and also of having done anything for the Government, the reward of which was not immediate and certain.

I sold my horses, my carriages, my furniture; I went bail for my brother who had contracted debts he was sure of paying, as he had several pictures on the easel which he had been ordered to paint by some of his rich and noble patrons. I took leave of Manon, whom I left in floods of tears, though I swore with the utmost sincerity to come back soon and marry her.

At last all my preparations were finished, and I left Paris with a hundred thousand francs in bills of exchange and jewels to the same amount. I was alone in my post-chaise, Le Duc preceding me on horseback, which the rascal preferred to being shut up in a carriage.

This Le Duc of mine was a Spaniard, aged eighteen, a sharp fellow, whom I valued highly, especially because he did my hair better than anyone else. I never refused him a pleasure which a little money would buy. Besides him I had a good Swiss servant, who served as my courier.

It was the 1st of December, 1759, and the air was frosty, but I was fortified against the inclemency of the season. I was able to read comfortably, and I took Helvetius's "Esprit," which I had never had time to read before. After perusing it I was equally astonished at the sensation it created and at the stupidity of the High Court which condemned it. Of course that exalted body was largely influenced by the king and the clergy, and between them all no effort was spared to ruin Helvetius, a good-hearted man with more wit than his book. I saw nothing novel either in the historical part relating to the morals of nations (in which Helvetius dismisses us as triflers), or in the position that morality is dependent on the reason. All that he says has been said over and over again, and Blaise Pascal went much farther, but he wrote more skilfully and better in every way than Helvetius, who, wishing to remain in France, was obliged to retract. He preferred a quiet life to his honour and his philosophy. His wife had a nobler soul than he, as she wanted to sell all they had, and to take refuge in Holland rather than submit to the shame of a recantation. Perhaps Helvetius would have followed the noble advice of his wife if he had foreseen that this monstrous recantation would make his book into a fraud; for he had to confess that he had written without due reflection, that he was more in jest than earnest, and that his arguments were mere sophisms. But many men of keen intellects had not waited for him to recant before exposing this wretched system of his. And admitting that whatever man does is done for his own interest, does it follow that gratitude is a folly, and virtue and vice identical? Are a villain and a man of honour to be weighed in the same balance? If such a dreadful system were not absurd, virtue would be mere hypocrisy; and if by any possibility it were true, it ought to be proscribed by general consent, since it would lead to general ruin and corruption.

It might have been proved to Helvetius that the propositions that the first motive is always self-interest, and that we should always consult our own interest first, are fallacious. It is a strange thing that so virtuous a man would not admit the existence of virtue. It is an amusing suggestion that he only published his book out of modesty, but that would have contradicted his own system. But if it were so, was it well done to render himself contemptible to escape the imputation of pride? Modesty is only a virtue when it is natural; if it is put on, or merely the result of training, it is detestable. The great d'Alembert was the most truly modest man I have ever seen.

When I got to Brussels, where I spent two days, I went to the "Hotel de l'Imperatrice," and chance sent Mdlle. X. C. V. and Farsetti in my way, but I pretended not to see them. From Brussels I went straight to the Hague, and got out at the "Prince of Orange." On my asking the host who sat down at his table, he told me his company consisted of general officers of the Hanoverian army, same English ladies, and a Prince Piccolomini and his wife; and this made me make up my mind to join this illustrious assemblage.

I was unknown to all, and keeping my eyes about me I gave my chief attention to the observation of the supposed Italian princess, who was pretty enough, and more especially of her husband whom I seemed to recognize. In the course of conversation I heard some talk of the celebrated St. Germain, and it seemed that he was stopping in the same hotel.

I had returned to my room, and was thinking of going to bed, when Prince Piccolomini entered, and embraced me as an old friend.

"A look in your face," said he, "tells me that the recognition has been mutual. I knew you directly in spite of the sixteen years that have passed since we saw each other at Vicenza. To-morrow you can tell everybody that we are friends, and that though I am not a prince I am really a count; here is my passport from the King of Naples, pray read it."

During this rapid monologue I could not get in a single word, and on attentively scanning his features I could only recollect that I had seen him before, but when or where or how I knew not. I opened the passport and read the name of Ruggero di Rocco, Count Piccolomini. That was enough; I remembered an individual of that name who was a fencing-master in Vicenza, and on looking at him again his aspect, though much changed left no doubt as to the identity of the swordsman and the count.

"I congratulate you," said I, "on your change of employment, your new business is doubtless much better than the old."

"I taught fencing," he replied, "to save myself from dying of hunger, for my father was so hard a man that he would not give me the wherewithal to live, and I disguised my name so as not to disgrace it. On my father's death I succeeded to the property, and at Rome I married the lady you have seen."

"You had good taste, for she's a pretty woman."

"She is generally thought so, and it was a love match on my side."

He ended by asking me to come and see him in his room the next day, after dinner, telling me that I should find good company and a bank at faro, which he kept himself. He added, without ceremony, that if I liked we could go half shares, and that I should find it profitable. I thanked him, and promised to pay him a visit.

I went abroad at an early hour next morning, and after having spent some time with the Jew, Boaz, and having given a polite refusal to his offer of a bed, I went to pay my respects to M. d'Afri, who since the death of the Princess of Orange, the Regent of the Low Countries, was generally known as His Most Christian Majesty's ambassador. He gave me an excellent reception, but he said that if I had returned to Holland hoping to do business on behalf of the Government I should waste my time, since the action of the comptroller-general had lowered the credit of the nation, which was thought to be on the verge of bankruptcy.

"This M. Silhouette," said he, "has served the king very badly. It is all very well to say that payments are only suspended for a year, but it is not believed."

He then asked me if I knew a certain Comte de St. Germain, who had lately arrived at the Hague.

"He has not called on me," said the ambassador, "though he says he is commissioned by the king to negotiate a loan of a hundred millions. When I am asked about him, I am obliged to say that I know nothing about him, for fear of compromising myself. Such a reply, as you can understand, is not likely to increase his chance of success, but that is his fault and not mine. Why has he not brought me a letter from the Duc de Choiseul or the Marquise de Pompadour? I take him to be an impostor, but I shall know something more about him in the course of ten days."

I told him, in my turn, all I knew of this truly eccentric individual. He was not a little surprised to hear that the king had given him an apartment at Chambord, but when I told him that the count professed to be able to make diamonds he laughed and said that in that case he would no doubt make the hundred millions. Just as I was leaving, M. d'Afri asked me to dine with him on the following day.

On returning to the hotel I called on the Comte de St. Germain.

"You have anticipated me," said he, on seeing me enter, "I intended to have called on you. I suppose, my dear Casanova, that you have come to try what you can do for our Court, but you will find your task a difficult one, as the Exchange is highly offended at the late doings of that fool Silhouette. All the same I hope I shall be able to get my hundred millions. I have passed my word to my friend, Louis XV (I may call him so), and I can't disappoint him; the business will be done in the next three or four weeks."

"I should think M. d'Afri might assist you."

"I do not require his assistance. Probably I shall not even call upon him, as he might say he helped me. No, I shall have all the trouble, and I mean to have all the glory, too."

"I presume you will be going to Court, where the Duke of Brunswick may be of service to you?"

"Why should I go to Court? As for the Duke of Brunswick, I do not care to know him. All I have got to do is to go to Amsterdam, where my credit is sufficiently good for anything. I am fond of the King of France; there's not a better man in the kingdom."

"Well, come and dine at the high table, the company is of the best and will please you."

"You know I never eat; moreover, I never sit down at a table where I may meet persons who are unknown to me."

"Then, my lord, farewell; we shall see each other again at Amsterdam."

I went down to the dining-roam, where, while dinner was being served, I conversed with some officers. They asked me if I knew Prince Piccolomini, to which I answered that he was not a prince but a count, and that it was many years since I had seen him.

When the count and his fair wife (who only spoke Italian) came down, I shewed them some polite attentions, and we then sat down to dinner.

A Note About the Author

Giacomo Casanova (1725–1798) was an Italian adventurer and author. Born in Venice, Casanova was the eldest of six siblings born to Gaetano Casanova and Zanetta Farussi, an actor and actress. Raised in a city noted for its cosmopolitanism, night life, and glamor, Casanova overcame a sickly childhood to excel in school, entering the University of Padua at the age of 12. After graduating in 1742 with a degree in law, he struggled to balance his work as a lawyer and low-level cleric with a growing gambling addiction. As scandals and a prison sentence threatened to derail his career in the church, Casanova managed to find work as a scribe for a powerful Cardinal in Rome, but was soon dismissed and entered military service for the Republic of Venice. Over the next several years, he left the service, succeeded as a professional gambler, and embarked on a Grand Tour of Europe. Towards the end of his life, Casanova worked on his exhaustive, scandalous memoirs, a 12-volume autobiography reflecting on a legendary life of romance and debauchery that brought him from the heights of aristocratic society to the lows of illness and imprisonment. Recognized for his self-styled sensationalism as much as he is for his detailed chronicling of 18th century European culture, Casanova is a man whose name is now synonymous with the kind of life he led—fast, fearless, and free.

A Note from the Publisher

Spanning many genres, from non-fiction essays to literature classics to children's books and lyric poetry, Mint Edition books showcase the master works of our time in a modern new package. The text is freshly typeset, is clean and easy to read, and features a new note about the author in each volume. Many books also include exclusive new introductory material. Every book boasts a striking new cover, which makes it as appropriate for collecting as it is for gift giving. Mint Edition books are only printed when a reader orders them, so natural resources are not wasted. We're proud that our books are never manufactured in excess and exist only in the exact quantity they need to be read and enjoyed.

bookfinity™

Discover more of your favorite classics with Bookfinity™.

- Track your reading with custom book lists.
- Get great book recommendations for your personalized Reader Type.
- Add reviews for your favorite books.
- AND MUCH MORE!

Visit **bookfinity.com** and take the fun Reader Type quiz to get started.

Enjoy our classic and modern companion pairings!

Classic & Modern

www.ingramcontent.com/pod-product-compliance
Lightning Source LLC
Chambersburg PA
CBHW021132020426
42331CB00005B/736